Dedicated to all parents everywhere.

www.gemmadenham.com

Published by Elizabeth Publications
Available from Amazon.com and other retail outlets
Available on Kindle and other devices

ISBN 978-0-9935579-4-1

Children's Party Planning

The complete guide for ages 1-10

Contents

Introduction

Children's parties, a joyful time of celebration, but also a stressful time for many parents. Gone are the days of having a few friends over for a jam sandwich and a game of pass the parcel, with many parents now going for extravagant events which usually include an expensive venue. But there is no need to panic. I am here to show you all that a home party has to give, and just how amazing they can be!

Firstly let me introduce myself. My name is Gemma, and I am a mother and avid party thrower! And when I say avid, I mean avid - I absolutely LOVE it! The whole kerbang! So much so that I am known to start my planning a good 6 months in advance of the actual event! Crazy as you may think that is, it means we have an absolutely awesome day, and it also means that I am able to save you all that hassle by writing this book.

This book contains a fantastic compilation of parties that will rival all others. With a whole range of different themes to choose from, each party covers invitations, food, decorations, games, party bags and of course the all important cake!

Fear not all you beginner crafters and bakers! For each make and bake there are clear simple step by step instructions and photographs to guide you along the way, and a range of pre-designed templates ready to download and use at **www.gemmadenham.com**. You will also find for each theme there are two cakes to choose from - an easy bake, or one for the more experienced baker.

Use this book as a guide and a trove of ideas and inspiration. You don't need to follow everything, and you also don't need to *make* everything either! Home-made food and decorations are great and they keep the costs down, but if it is really not your thing, and the thought of it fills you with dread then shop bought is worth every penny. A party after all is a fun time, and should be for everyone!

1st Birthday

1 year old, *a whole year!* How did that happen! Whilst this is a huge deal for you, it is important to remember that your child will be largely unaware, and a huge party will only serve to overwhelm. Keep it simple - small is definitely beautiful at this age!

A few tips:

• Take into consideration your child's nap time. Plan the party for pre or post nap, when you know your baby won't be tired!

• Keep the guest list small, so as not to overwhelm.

• Simple finger food that can be eaten on the go is ideal as eating them won't interrupt play - a sit down party tea is not very realistic for this age.

• Home is where your baby will be most comfortable, so it is the ideal location to hold your party. It also means that you can't forget to take anything with you when baby brain hits!

• The parents will stay with the children for a party of this age, so have plenty of chairs around for the grown-ups, and some tea and coffee available. Remember though, that this is a children's party, and you don't have to cater for the adults too, offering a drink is sufficient.

Freya is turning 1

Please join us in celebrating

On Sunday 15th January
10.30 – 11.30am

At Freya's House

R.S.V.P Freya's mummy 01234567891

The invitation

How cute is this! And so easy to make! Print out all your details for the party on some good quality card, tie a ribbon around a cake candle and stick to the invite with a blob of PVA glue. *Voila!*

Choosing a theme

Party themes aren't important to a 1 year old, it's more for the benefit of the photographs at this stage, so you may just wish to go for a colour coordinated look.

Party bags

It's up to you whether or not to give out party bags. At this age I don't think it's expected, and a piece of wrapped Birthday cake is more than sufficient. But, if you do want to, here are some ideas.

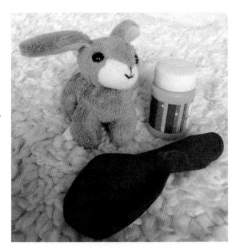

- Mini bubbles
- Balloon
- Small toy
- Raisin boxes
- Small bag of biscuits
- Mini board book
- Musical instrument
- Chocolate buttons

The activities

The majority of your guest list will still be crawling, so have lots of floor play zones, and make use of all the toys and equipment you have.

- A selection of toys and building blocks.

- Fill a paddling pool with balls for a mini ball pit.

- Pop up play tents and tunnels.

- Lots of colourful balloons! Although please note that a popped balloon is a choking hazard! Be careful to remove all the remnants of a popped balloon as quickly as possible.

- Bubbles! Bubble machines are fairly inexpensive and are always a huge hit!

Decorate the room with bunting and balloons (details on how to make your own bunting on page 55 and 67) and have a little music playing in the background.

If you wanted to add a bit of structure to the party, how about a sing-a-long? Gather everyone round into a circle, and sing some of your favourite action songs - row, row, row the boat, twinkle twinkle little star, wheels on the bus etc.

Rainbow Cake -Easy

For each layer you will need:
100g (4oz) butter or margarine
100g (4oz) caster sugar
2 medium eggs
100g (4oz) self raising flour
Food colouring

For the buttercream:
250g butter or margarine
500 sifted icing sugar
Few drops vanilla or
lemon essence (optional)

1. Preheat the oven to 180°c, 350°f, gas mark 4. Grease a 7 inch round cake tin, and line the bottom.

2. Cream the butter and sugar until light and fluffy. Beat in the eggs, and add the food colouring according to the manufacturers instructions.

3. Gently fold in the flour and pour into the prepared tin.

4. Bake for 40-45 minutes. The cake is fully cooked when a skewer inserted in the centre comes out clean.

Repeat the above until you have 4 differently coloured cakes.

5. To make the buttercream - cream the butter, gradually add the icing sugar and cream together. Add the flavouring if you are using.

6. Using a cake cutting wire, or a bread knife, slice the top off each cake to give you a flat level surface. Put of blob of icing onto a cake board, and place on your 1st cake layer.

7. Cover with a little buttercream, then add the 2nd cake. Repeat until you have all 4 layers.

8. Cover the sides and top of the cake with a thin layer of buttercream, refrigerate for 30 mins. (This will seal the cake and stop cake crumbs from mixing with the final finish)

9. Cover the cake with the remaining buttercream (don't worry if you can't get it smooth! A rough finish will look just as good), and add some sprinkles to the top.

Bunting Cake – Moderate

You will need:

275g (10oz) butter or margarine
275g (10oz) caster sugar
5 medium eggs
275g (10oz) self raising flour

For decorating:

75g butter or margarine
150 sifted icing sugar
600g white ready roll icing
Food colouring
Lolly stick and ribbon

1. Preheat the oven to 180°c, 350°f, gas mark 4. Grease two 6 inch round cake tins, and line the bottom.

2. Cream the butter and sugar until light and fluffy. Beat in the eggs, and then gently fold in the flour.

3. Pour into the prepared tins, and bake for 40-45 minutes. The cake is fully cooked when a skewer inserted in the centre comes out clean.

4. To make the buttercream - cream the butter, gradually add the icing sugar, and cream together.

5. Using a cake cutting wire, or bread knife, slice the top off each cake to give you a flat level surface. Sandwich and cover with buttercream and ready roll icing as shown on page 167.

6. Using a small bowl, or large cookie cutter, gently push into the side of the cake all the way around, to give you a guideline for the bunting to follow.

7. With the off cuts of icing, roll out several long fine strings. Paint along the guideline with a little water, or edible glue, then, gently press a string of icing onto it, cutting off any excess at the top. Repeat until you have covered all the guidelines.

8. Split the remaining icing into 3, and knead in a few drops of food colouring (a different colour into each) until fully mixed. Cut into triangles, and stick along the strings.

9. Cut 2 identical hearts (or other shape) of the same colour, and 1 slightly bigger heart of a different colour. In the bigger heart, cut a slot to fit your lolly stick, then stick a smaller heart to the front and back. Leave this out over night to harden. Once set, pipe on the number and stick into the centre of the cake.

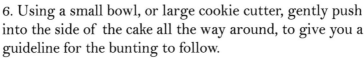

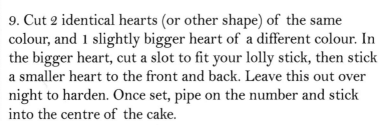

2 - 4 year olds

Children in this age group benefit from a good strong theme - it helps to keep attention spans focused! A party for 2-4 year olds usually lasts about 1 1/2 hours.

A few tips:

• Toddlers can become quickly overwhelmed by having a lot of people around all at once, so try to keep things small still, anywhere up to 8 friends.

• Some children of this age will still be taking afternoon naps, so bear this in mind when planning your party. Mornings or lunchtime will probably work best.

• Home is still the best place if you have the room, or alternatively a small village hall.

• Toddlers are not good losers! So if you are thinking of handing out prizes, it might be best to award participation rather than an overall winner.

• Children of this age may have trouble taking turns. The teddy bears picnic and dinosaur parties are perfect themes for 2 year olds as the games listed for these parties are all group activities. For the other parties in this section alternate group games with those that require turn taking.

• If the children are becoming restless, interspace the games with a little free play to let them run around and blow off some steam! You will probably only need 2 or 3 of the games listed for the younger of the ages, so do your favourites 1st.

Teddy Bears' Picnic

The invitation

Impressive, yet very simple to make. You will need some patterned card cut into squares of about 15cm x 15cm, some lengths of thin ribbon, and some brown card.

For a simple version, leave the text off the front. Print (or write) your invite details onto the back of the patterned card. Draw around a teddy cookie cutter onto the brown card, cut out the bears, tie a bow around the neck, and stick to the patterned base with a little PVA.

If you are feeling a little more adventurous and are confident on a computer, find and download an online bear template, type your text to fit inside and print out onto the brown card. Finish as above.

Setting the theme

What better way to welcome your guests into your party. Create a paw print stencil by cutting some circles out of some thick card, then simply sieve a little flour over the top for a paw print walkway leading the way. A handwritten sign post finishes the look.

19

The Games

The great thing about a teddy bears picnic, is that it can be as simple as just that - everyone turning up with a bear, sitting out on blankets and having a picnic. If the weather is in your favour, then the world is your oyster as far as location goes - the garden, local park or woodland all provide the perfect backdrop. If the weather or time of year means outdoors is not an option, simply clear the living room, and lay down blankets and cushions for a cosy setting.

If you are not planning on playing any games, make sure you have plenty of toys out to keep everyone amused after the food, and bear in mind that some children will undoubtedly forget to bring a bear, so have some spares and other soft toys handy to avoid tears!

If you are ready to take on the challenge of party games, then here some good themed ones to get the party going.

Craft table

Craft activities are hugely popular with this age group, so set up a craft table with paints and crayons where they can get creative and make a bear mask or decorate some binoculars ready for the bear hunt.

Bear hunt

Grab some teddy bear cutouts and tape to sticks. Hide them around the garden, or if having indoors, stickytac them around the room.
Using your binoculars, see how many you can find.

Teddy bear race

Grab a teddy, hold him onto your shoulders, and race!
Or, how about racing like a teddy bear - get onto all fours and run like a bear!
Only have a small space? Then make it a relay. Ready, teddy, GO!

Story time

A great calm down before the food is handed out. Gather everyone together onto picnic blankets and read them one of your favourite bear stories. Bring the food out at the end whilst everyone is still seated.

Pass the bear

Everyone sits in a circle around the honey pot (a tea canister or biscuit tin labelled as 'honey' works well). When the music plays, you pass the bear. When the music stops, the person holding the teddy takes a treat from the honey pot. Make sure every child has a go at taking a treat!

The Food

Continue your theme through the food to tempt even the fussiest eater! Individually bagged picnics are not only cute, but cut out a whole lot of stress! For each child, fill a paper bag with a couple of sandwiches (cut into teddy shapes), a piece of fruit, a gingerbread bear and a carton of juice. Bringing the cakes out separately *after* the children are finished with the main picnic will encourage better eating!

Paw print cupcakes

100g (4oz) butter
100g (4oz) caster sugar
2 medium eggs
100g (4oz) self raising flour

1. Preheat the oven to 190°c, 375°f, gas mark 5.
2. Cream the butter and sugar until light and fluffy.
3. Beat in the eggs, 1 at a time.
4. Gently fold in the flour.
5. Pour into 12 paper cases and bake for 15-20 minutes.
6. Top with a swirl of buttercream. A giant chocolate button and 3 chocolate raisins make the paw.

Chocy marshmallow bears

100g (4oz) milk chocolate
12 x marshmallows
12 x mini bear biscuits
12 x wooden skewers

1. Break the chocolate into pieces and melt in a bowl over a pan of simmering water. Remove from the heat.
2. Skewer a marshmallow, and dip into the melted chocolate.
3. Put a little chocolate onto the back of a bear to stick it to the marshmallow.
Leave to set.

Gingerbread bears

300g (10oz) self raising flour
3 tsp ground ginger
100g (4oz) sugar
50g (2oz) butter/margarine
3tbsp goldern syrup
4 tbsp milk

1. Preheat oven to 160°c, 325°f, gas mark 3.
2. Warm sugar, fat and syrup then add the dry ingredients.
3. Add milk & mix until firm.
4. Roll out & cut using a teddy cutter. Place onto a greased tray & bake for 10-15 minutes. Decorate with icing and chocolate buttons once cool.

Teddy Cake - Easy

For the head:
175g (6oz) butter or margarine
175g (6oz) caster sugar
3 medium eggs
150g (5oz) self raising flour
25g (1oz) cocoa powder

For the ears and muzzle:
100g (4oz) butter or margarine
100g (4oz) caster sugar
2 medium eggs
75g (3oz) self raising flour
25g (1oz) cocoa powder

For decorating:
185g (8oz) butter or margarine
375g (15oz) sifted icing sugar
25g (1oz) cocoa powder
chocolate buttons or fondant

1. Preheat the oven to 180°c, 350°f, gas mark 4. Grease a 7 inch round cake tin to be the head, and line the bottom.

2. Cream the butter and sugar until light and fluffy. Beat in the eggs, and then gently fold in the flour and cocoa.

3. Pour into the prepared tin, and bake for 45-50 minutes. The cake is fully cooked when a skewer inserted in the centre comes out clean.

4. The ears and muzzle can be cut to size from a small tin, we used a 6 x 3.5 inch loaf tin (which we cut the 2 ears from), and a 3.25 inch round tin for the muzzle. Make up the cake(s) as above, and bake for 35-40 minutes.

5. To make the buttercream - cream the butter, gradually add the icing sugar, and cream together.

6. Using a cake wire, or bread knife, slice the top off each cake to give you a flat level surface.

7. Using a little buttercream, stick the cake pieces to the board, and the muzzle into position. Cover the muzzle and inner ears in buttercream.

8. Add the cocoa to the remaining buttercream and mix well. Thinly cover the rest of the exposed cake.

9. Fit a piping bag with a no.233 piping nozzle (grass/hair nozzle), and fill with the buttercream.

10. Holding the bag straight up, squeeze and pull up and away to create a fur effect, or alternatively, create a random pattern by squeezing and wiggling.

11. Change the piping tip to a fine point to ice on the smile. Top with chocolate buttons to create the eyes and nose.

Teddy Cake – Moderate

You will need:

200g (8oz) butter or margarine
200g (8oz) caster sugar
4 medium eggs
200g (8oz) self raising flour

For decorating:

50g (2oz) butter or margarine
100g (4oz) sifted icing sugar
500g (20oz) white ready roll icing
Food colouring
50g (2oz) brown icing

1. Preheat the oven to 180°c, 350°f, gas mark 4. Grease two 6 inch round cake tins, and line the bottom.

2. Cream the butter and sugar until light and fluffy. Beat in the eggs, and then gently fold in the flour.

3. Pour into the prepared tins, and bake for 40-45 minutes. The cake is fully cooked when a skewer inserted in the centre comes out clean.

4. To make the buttercream - cream the butter, gradually add the icing sugar, and cream together.

5. Using a cake cutting wire, or bread knife, slice the top off each cake to give you a flat level surface.

6. Use a blob of buttercream to stick the cake to the board. Cover the top with buttercream, then add the 2nd cake, cut side down.

7. Cover the entire cake with a thin layer of buttercream.

8. Knead the icing until pliable. Roll out to a thickness of about 5mm. Using your cake tin as a template - cut out a circle and set aside.

9. Split the remaining icing into 3 balls and knead a little of your chosen food colouring into each to give you 3 different colours.

10. Roll out each colour thinly, and cut into 2cm strips.

11. Stick the coloured strips in a repeating pattern around the sides of the cake. Cut each strip at the top level with the cake, and smooth the sides where each colour joins.

12. Top the cake with the earlier prepared white circle.

Continued.....

Making teddy:

1. Take the brown icing and knead until pliable. Split into 2 equal balls.

2. Take 3/4 of the 1st ball. Roll into a ball, then placing onto your work surface, work the top upwards with your fingers to create a pear shape. This will be the body.

3. With the remainder of the 1st ball, split into 2 and roll into sausage shapes. Gently squeeze in at one end of each to create a slight tear drop. Flatten out the other end (to create paws). These will be the arms.

4. Take 1/2 of the 2nd ball. Pinch off a little to use for ears and set aside. Roll the rest into 2 equal sausage shapes. Holding upright, gently push each one down onto your worktop whilst tapering in the top with your fingers. These will be the legs.

5. Roll the remainder of the 2nd ball to form the head.

6. Using the off cuts of one of the side colours from the cake, roll and flatten small balls to create the paws, inner ears and muzzle. Stick to the main body pieces with a little edible glue or water.

7. Using a cocktail stick, indent a line down each body piece to create the stitching effect, then assemble the bear on top of the cake.

Party bags

Keep your theme going right to the end with these adorable party bags. Very simply (and cheaply) made with wrapping paper and a paper bag, but the end result as I'm sure you will agree, has so much more quality to it than shop bought plastic ones!

Fill with anything bear related:

- Gummy bears
- A choccy marshmallow bear lolly
- Colouring book and crayons (see below)
- Small stuffed bear
- Stickers

This bag also has plenty of room to fit the mask and/or binocular make, and don't forget a piece of the yummy Birthday cake!

Making a colouring book

A good addition to any party bag, and a lot simpler to make than you may think! If you have an artistic side then you can draw your own pictures, otherwise there are plenty of free colouring pages online that you can download. You want to fit 4 pictures to a piece of A4, and have at least 2 sheets (so 8 images). Print out your pictures, and cut into the separate pages. You will also need a piece of card of the same size for the back, and a patterned piece for the cover. Staple all of these together, then glue a strip of paper on top of these (front, back and spine) to hide the staples.

Fairy tea party

The invitation

So pretty and so perfect, what little fairy could resist!

Type (or write) you invitation into a star shape and cut out. On some patterned card cut out a slightly larger star. Glue the 2 stars together with a wooden dowel or paper straw in the centre. Tie some ribbon to the top. *Voila!*

The Games

~Lily pad leap~

You will need 4 big lily pads (these can be cushions or some coloured card) and 2 teams. Played as a relay race, each team has 2 lily pads and must use them to cross the floor by standing on 1, moving the other infront and leaping onto it, repeating until they reach the other side. The winning team is the 1st to cross all their fairies.

~Find the butterflies~

You will need some large pebbles, patterned card cut into butterfly shapes, glue and glitter. Cover the top of each pebble with glue and sprinkle on some glitter, then with a good blob of PVA stick on a butterfly. Hide around the house/garden for your fairies to find. You may find your guests wanting to take these home, so make enough for 1 each!

~Sleeping fairies~

Lie all your little fairies down on the floor with their eyes closed as if they are asleep. One fairy moves around trying to wake them by getting them to move or laugh (without touching!). Any fairies that wake can join in the waking. The last fairy asleep is the winner.

~Fairy tea relay~

This one can get messy, so it's best played outside! Divide your fairies into 2 teams. Give each team an empty teapot and a cup, and at the other end of the garden have 2 bowls filled with water. The idea of the game is to race to the bucket, fill the cup and carry it back to fill the teapot. The 1st team to fill their pot wins.

~Decorate fairy cakes~

A great activity that can double as a party bag gift. You will need 1 plain cupcake per fairy. Set up a table with icing and sprinkles and let them go to work. Cake toppers are a good idea and easy way to label the cakes at the end. Print out some fairy pictures, write/type on a name and attach to a cocktail stick.

The Food

A picnic tea fit for a fairy! It's amazing how a few simple measures can transform an ordinary picnic into something that little bit special! Sandwiches cut with a butterfly cutter into delicate bite sized portions, crisps served in teacups and salad cut into flowers served alongside these special sweet treats all pull together to make this fairy tea magical!

Butterfly Cupcakes

100g (4oz) butter
100g (4oz) caster sugar
2 medium eggs
100g (4oz) self raising flour

1. Preheat the oven to 190°c, 375°f, gas mark 5.
2. Cream the butter and sugar until light and fluffy.
3. Beat in the eggs, 1 at a time.
4. Gently fold in the flour.
5. Pour into 12 paper cases and bake for 15-20 minutes.
6. When cool, slice the top off each cake, cut this in half.
7. Swirl a little buttercream on each cake, and arrange the 'wings'.

Toadstool lollies

12 x strawberries
12 x marshmallows
12 x wooden skewers
2 tbsp icing sugar

1. Cut the tops off the strawberries to remove the stalk.
2. Push a marshmallow onto a skewer, followed by a strawberry - cut end 1st.
3. Mix the icing sugar with a little water to form a thick paste, and pipe little blobs around the strawberry.

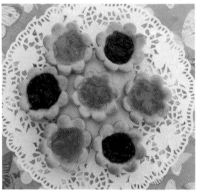

Flower tarts

100g (4oz) plain flour
50g (2oz) margarine
Cold water to mix (approx. 2 tbsp)
Jam and lemon curd

1. Preheat oven to 200°c, 400°f, gas mark 6.
2. Place the flour in a bowl and rub in the margarine.
3. Using a knife to stir, mix in the water (a little at a time) to form a stiff dough.
4. Roll out thinly, and cut with a flower cutter. Place in greased patty tins.
5. Fill with a little jam or lemon, bake for 15 minutes.

35

Fairy Cake - Easy

You will need:

350g (12oz) butter or margarine
350g (12oz) caster sugar
6 medium eggs
350g (12oz) self raising flour

For decorating:

125g (5oz) butter or margarine
250g (10oz) sifted icing sugar
100g (4oz) white fondant
Food colouring
Fairy figurine and sprinkles

1. Preheat the oven to 180°c, 350°f, gas mark 4. Grease two 7 inch round cake tins, and line the bottom.

2. Cream the butter and sugar until light and fluffy. Beat in the eggs, and then gently fold in the flour.

3. Pour into the prepared tins, and bake for 40-45 minutes. The cake is fully cooked when a skewer inserted in the centre comes out clean.

4. To make the buttercream - cream the butter, gradually add the icing sugar and cream together.

5. Slowly add some pink/red food colouring a little at a time to the buttercream, until you get the desired shade. Mix well.

6. Using a cake wire, or bread knife, slice the top off each cake to give you a flat level surface. Use a blob of buttercream to stick the cake to the cake board, sandwiching the two cakes with a generous amount of buttercream.

7. Cover the entire cake with a thin layer of buttercream, and chill in the fridge for at least 30 minutes (This will seal the cake, and stop crumbs mixing with the final layer). Once set, cover with the remaining buttercream. Don't worry if you find a smooth finish difficult to acheive, this works just as well with a rough finish.

8. Add a circle of sprinkles around the top of the cake. Roll out the white fondant thinly and cut with a flower cutter. Arrange around the base of the cake.

9. Mix a little icing sugar with yellow food colouring, slowly adding a little water until you have a thick pipable consistancy. Pipe into the centre of each flower.

Toadstool Cake – For the experienced baker

For each stalk layer:
50g (2oz) butter or margarine
50g (2oz) caster sugar
1 medium egg
50g (2oz) self raising flour

For the top:
175g (6oz) butter or margarine
175g (6oz) caster sugar
3 medium eggs
175g (6oz) self raising flour

For decorating:
200g (8oz) sifted icing sugar
100g (4oz) butter/margarine
1tbsp cocoa powder
Green food colouring
300g (12oz) white fondant
300g (12oz) red fondant
25g (1oz) brown fondant
25g (1oz) purple fondant

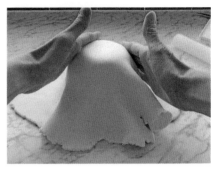

1. Preheat the oven to 180°c, 350°f, gas mark 4. For the stalk use a 4.5 inch round cake tin.

2. Cream the butter and sugar until light and fluffy. Beat in the egg, and then gently fold in the flour.

3. Pour into the prepared tin, and bake for 40 minutes. The cake is fully cooked when a skewer inserted in the centre comes out clean. Repeat until you have 3 layers.

4. For the top, use a 6 inch round cake tin. Grease, line and prepare using the above method. Bake for 45-50 minutes.

5. To make the buttercream - cream the butter, gradually add the icing sugar, and cream together. Separate into 3 bowls - 120g plain, 50g mixed with the cocoa and the remaining 30g coloured green.

6. Sandwich the stalk cake layers with a generous amount of plain buttercream. Taper the top by cutting away the corners in a circular motion around the cake.

7. Cover the stalk in a thin layer of plain buttercream, and cover with white fondant as shown on page 167.

8. Thinly roll out the brown and purple fondant. Cut into arches (as shown left) to make the windows and doors. Use a knife to indent the brown for the wood effect.

38

Continued.....

9. Using edible glue or a little water, stick the windows and door onto the stalk.

10. Take the green buttercream, and spread around the base of the stalk and the cake board. Use a fork to create a grass effect.

11. With the top cake, cut away the corners in a circular motion around the cake. You are looking to create a dome shape.

12. Spread the bottom of the cake with the chocolate buttercream. Once covered, drag a fork from the centre to the edge of the cake. Continue all the way around to create the underside 'ruffle' of the toadstool. Place on top of the stalk.

13. Cover the top in a thin layer of plain buttercream, and cover with red fondant as shown on page 167. Trim the overhanging edges.

14. Thinly roll out the off cuts of white fondant. Cut circles, and stick to the top of the cake. Make sure some of them overhang, cut to fit the top.

15. With the remnants of purple, white and red, roll thinly and cut with a small flower cutter. Place these on the grass around the base of the cake. With the brown fondant make stepping stones leading to the door, by cutting out small squares.

Party bags

Break the boundaries of the party bag with these captured fairies. Not only are they cute as a button, but they are very easy to make and won't break the bank either!

Choose between natural fairies for a woodland look, and sweet treat fairies to incorporate a treat along with a gift. Both I'm sure you will agree are simply magical.

You will need:
1 empty washed out jar (with lid) and 1 fairy doll/figurine per child, some fabric cut into 10cm x 10cm squares and some ribbon.

If you are making natural fairies you will need dried moss and glitter, and if you are making sweet treat fairies you will need a selection of small sweets.

Natural Fairy

Place a little dried moss at the bottom of the jar, press down and place a fairy on top.
Add a little more of the moss around her feet, then sprinkle with plenty of glitter.
Screw on the lid, cover with a square of fabric, and tie into place with some ribbon.

Sweet treat Fairy

Cover the bottom of the jar with a handful of small sweets and sit your fairy on top.
Screw on the lid, cover with a square of fabric, and tie into place with some ribbon.

The invitation

Wow your party guests before they even arrive with these 3D dino invitations.

All you will need is some coloured card and googly eyes.

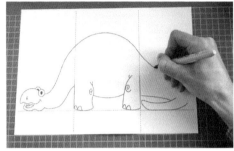

You will find a downloadable template of this dinosaur at **www.gemmadenham.com** or if you want to create your own design, then just follow these simple steps:

1. Take a piece of A4 paper and fold into 3 sections.

2. Draw your dinosaur with the head in the 1st section, body and legs in the 2nd, and tail in the 3rd.

Important: Make sure that there is at least part of your design touching the bottom in all 3 sections. This will ensure your invite stands once folded!

3. Once you are happy with the design, scan or photocopy it onto some coloured card. (If you are handy with a computer you can type your invite details on the body section before printing out.)

4. Fold along the section lines so the invite zigzags, glue on a googly eye and *Voila!*

Setting the theme

Very simple, but very effective! Make up some dinosaur warning signs by printing out silhouettes onto yellow card. Attach a garden cane to the back with sticky tape and place around the garden, or along the walkway to your party.

Have plenty of dinosaurs out to keep your guests amused whilst they wait for everyone to arrive.

43

The Games

~Fossil dig~

Become real dino explorers with this fossil hunt game.

Fill a box or deep tray with compost or sand and hide your fossils for the explorers to find. The fossils can be made from salt dough (see below) or be shells or even toy dinosaurs. Provide trowels, paintbrushes and sieves for the ultimate archaeologist experience!

Salt dough is made by mixing 1 cup flour, with 1/2 cup salt and 1/2 cup water. Form into bone shapes, or create 'fossils' by pressing with toy dinosaurs and shells. Leave to air dry for 2-3 days, or pop them in the oven on the lowest heat for 2-3 hours.

~Egg hunt~

Take 2 cups plain flour, 1 cup salt, 1 cup ground coffee and 1 cup water. Combine to form a soft dough, and form into an egg shape around a small plastic dinosaur. Leave to dry for 2-3 days. Hide them around the room or garden for the children to find and 'hatch'.

~Dino egg & spoon Race~

Once each child has found an egg, why not use them to have an egg and spoon race with before you hatch them.

~Dinosaur Cave~

Set up a prehistoric camp using a tent or dark coloured sheets over a table. Fill with a few props such as binoculars, dinosaurs, explorer hats etc. and let their imaginations run wild!

~Cave drawings~

Pin or tack a large piece of black card to the wall or fence. Hand out some chalks for your little dinosaur hunters to create some prehistoric cave drawings.

~Dino egg toss~

Grab some plastic eggs or make your own bean bag ones (shown right). Create a nest by surrounding a bowl with sticks and see who can toss the eggs inside.

FOSSIL DIG

The Food

What a prehistoric feast! Add a little 'dino' fun to your sandwiches by cutting with a dinosaur cookie cutter. Serve alongside some breaded chicken dinosaurs, and jungle veggie sticks. Add our dinosaur eggs and footprint cookies for that extra special touch.

Dinosaur eggs

6 eggs
food colouring
carrot

1. Place the eggs into a saucepan full of water.
2. Bring to the boil, then simmer for 10 minutes.
3. Remove from the heat, and cool in cold water.
4. Once cold, crack the shells all over.
5. Place in a bowl of cold water with approx. 1 tbsp of food colouring. Leave to stand for at least 8 hours.
6. Remove the shells and serve in a 'nest' of grated carrot.

Footprint Cookies

225g (8oz) butter or margarine
110g (4oz) sugar
275g (10oz) plain flour
Plastic dinosaurs

1. Preheat the oven to 180°c, 350°f, gas mark 4.
2. Cream the butter and sugar until light and fluffy.
3. Sift in the flour, and mix to form a firm dough.
4. Dip the dinosaur feet into plain flour, then press into the top of each biscuit.
5. Bake for 15 minutes.
6. Leave plain, or fill the footprints with icing.

DINOSAUR CAKE — *Easy*

You will need:
200g (8oz) butter or margarine
200g (8oz) caster sugar
4 medium eggs
175g (7oz) self raising flour
25g (2oz) cocoa powder

For decorating:
125g (5oz) butter or margarine
250g (10oz) sifted icing sugar
50g (2oz) cocoa powder
green food colouring

1. Preheat the oven to 180°c, 350°f, gas mark 4. Grease two 6 inch round cake tins, and line the bottom.

2. Cream the butter and sugar until light and fluffy. Beat in the eggs, and then gently fold in the flour and cocoa.

3. Pour into the prepared tins, and bake for 40-45 minutes. The cake is fully cooked when a skewer inserted in the centre comes out clean.

4. To make the chocolate buttercream - cream 75g (3oz) butter with 150g (6oz) sifted icing sugar and the cocoa.

5. Using a cake cutting wire, or bread knife, slice the top off each cake to give you a flat level surface.

6. Use a blob of chocolate buttercream to stick the cake to the board. Cover the top with buttercream, then add the 2nd cake, cut side down. Cover the sides of the cake with the remaining buttercream.

7. Hold a fork against the side of the cake. Keeping the fork steady, slowly rotate the cake to leave running indentations around the entire cake. Repeat further up until the whole side of the cake is covered all the way around.

8. To make the green buttercream - cream 50g (2oz) butter with 100g (4oz) sifted icing sugar and the green food colouring. Fit a piping bag with a no.233 piping nozzle (grass/hair nozzle), and fill with the buttercream.

9. Starting around the edges and working in- squeeze, pull and release the icing bag to create the grass effect. Arrange plastic dinosaurs on top.

You will need:

350g (12oz) butter or margarine
350g (12oz) caster sugar
6 medium eggs
350g (12oz) self raising flour

For decorating:

50g (2oz) butter or margarine
100g (4oz) sifted icing sugar
500g (20oz) green fondant
25g (1oz) purple fondant
White fondant or white
chocolate buttons for eyes

1. Preheat the oven to 180°c, 350°f, gas mark 4.
Grease two 7 inch round cake tins, and line the bottom.

2. Cream the butter and sugar until light and fluffy. Beat in the eggs, and then gently fold in the flour.

3. Pour into the prepared tins, and bake for 40-45 minutes. The cake is fully cooked when a skewer inserted in the centre comes out clean.

4. To make the buttercream - cream the butter with the sifted icing sugar.

5. Using a bread knife, cut one of the cakes in half. Sandwich together with a generous amount of buttercream, and stick to the cake board.

6. Cut the corner edges off this on both sides as shown above. This will be the body of the dinosaur.

7. Take the 2nd cake and cut in half. Divide the cake up and cut into the sections as shown left.

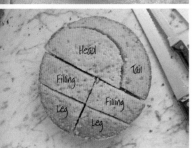

8. Stick the pieces in position on the cake board with a little buttercream, and trim to shape.

Take your time shaping the cake. Think of it more as shaving with the knife rather than cutting. Use the pieces labelled 'filling' to bridge the gap between the head and the body, and the tail and the body. Remember - any bumps or gaps will show in the icing, so try and get the shape as smooth as possible.

  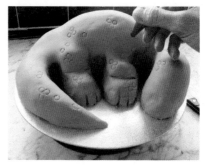

9. Knead the green fondant until pliable and roll out to about 4–5mm thick. Make sure it is large enough to cover the whole cake!

10. Lift the fondant, either using your forearms or the rolling pin, and drape over the cake. Shape and smooth with your hands around the body, tail and head. Cut the excess at the bottom of these areas to fit.

11. Slit the fondant between the legs/tail/head. Smooth over the sides of these areas - around the tail and head there should be enough fondant to pull down and cover to the board.

12. Cut semi circles of fondant to fill the gaps between the legs and board. Carefully stick these in place, and smooth over the join - 1st with a fondant tool, then with your fingers. After careful rubbing and smoothing the join should disappear.

13. Using different sizes of circular ended piping nozzles - indent the cake in a random pattern to create scales (you can also use this to disguise any visable join that's left).

14. Thinly roll out the purple fondant, and cut out the spikes or plates. You will need these to be of graduating sizes - they start small on the head, getting bigger as they go up onto the back, then getting smaller again onto and down the tail.

15. Paint a line of edible glue or water along the centre of the head, back and tail, and stick the plates into place.

16. Cut 2 circles of white for eyes and stick onto the face. Indent nostrils and a mouth.

DINOSAUR EGGS

THANK YOU FOR
COMING TO MY PARTY!

If you would like to make your own design, you will need to do so on a piece of card measuring 10.5cm long x 10cm high. Remember that the bottom half of this will be the front, and the top half will be folded over to make the back (so any design you do on the top half will need to be upside down).

Excavation favours

A little more money in the party bag budget? Then how about these excavation party favours.

You will need a plastic bucket and spade for each child. Fill with your choice of 'excavation' items such as paintbrushes, dinosaur sand moulds, magnifying glass etc. You could also add in little extras such as colouring/activity books and stickers.

Party bags

How 'roarsome' are these little party bags! A simple idea that has a big impact. These dinosaur egg bags incorporate everything you want from a party bag in a very easy to make effective way.

You will need:
4" x 6" grip seal polythene candy bags
chocolate mini eggs and/or jelly beans
plastic dinosaurs

Half fill the bags with sweets, pop in a little plastic dinosaur, and seal. Fold the banner card (details below) in half lengthways, and staple to the top of the bag.

Making the banner card
The banner card shown left can be download from **www.gemmadenham.com**. Print out on glossy paper/card and attach as above.

FUNFAIR PARTY

The invitation

What else could the invite for a funfair party be than a funfair flyer!

You will find a downloadable template of this flyer at **www.gemmadenham.com** for you to type or write your own details onto, or get creative and have a go at designing your own. Print out onto a good quality or photo finish paper for a more authentic look.

Voila!

Setting the theme

Balloons and bunting set the theme for a funfair party, you want to get as much colour around as possible! Bunting is fairly cheap to buy and readily available, but it is also very easy to make yourself.

Making bunting

You will need:
Different coloured fabric (off cuts & scraps will do)
Cotton tape
Pinking shears & pins

1. Draw a triangle onto some card and cut it out to use as a template.
2. Pin the template to the fabric, and cut around it using the pinking shears. Repeat until you have enough flags for the length of bunting you are making.
3. Pin the flags along the length of the tape, and sew into place. Make sure you leave some length of tape free at each end for tying!

The Games

This is a brilliant party to add fancy dress and face paints to!
For a true funfair feel create 'lucky dip' prizes - wrap a shoe box in colourful paper (box and lid separately) and cut a large circle out of the top. Fill with sawdust or paper shreddings, and hide small wrapped prizes inside. Once everyone has had a go at the game let them pick out a prize.

~Hook a duck~

No funfair is complete without hook a duck! Play this outside by filling a paddling pool with water (inside use a large bowl). Screw small hooks into the top of some plastic ducks, and larger hooks into the end of garden canes. If you manage to hook a duck you win!

~Tin can alley~

Cover 6 washed out tin cans (make sure there are no sharp bits left on the opening) with wrapping paper. Stack into a pyramid, and take turns at trying to knock them all down with a tennis ball. After a few practice shots try setting the distance further away!

~Ring toss~

The idea of ring toss is to throw your ring around a peg. You can buy these as sets, or create your own with a wooden stake pushed into the garden, or a clear plastic bottle filled with coloured water as the peg. Cut rings out of thick, stiff card and bind with twine.

~Coconut shy~

Whilst coconuts are easily and cheaply found, the metal pins can be very expensive! Try our home-made version using painted plastic piping or snack tubes. Push the piping into plant pots or the garden to keep steady. Snack tubes will sit on any level surface, though you may want to weigh them down. Place a coconut on top of each, and use bean bags to try and knock them off.

~Pin the tail on the donkey~

You will need a picture of a donkey with a missing tail, a tail for each child and a blindfold. Tack the donkey to a wall, and apply double sided tape to one end of each tail. One at a time, each child is blindfolded and handed a 'tail'. The winner is the closest to the correct position.

~Ball in the bucket~

Throw the balls into the bucket and if they stay in there you're a winner!
This game just requires a large piece of painted corrugated card to surround your bucket. Cut a hole in the middle to slot the bucket into, and you're all set!

BALL IN THE
BUCKET

LUCKY DIP

The Food

All the fun of the fair with these carnival treats!
Serve burgers and hot dogs along with popcorn cones and chocolate apples for that true funfair feel. The chocolate apples are also great to bag up and offer as a party bag extra.

Cholly top apples

150g (6oz) milk chocolate
6 small apples
sprinkles
wooden skewers

1. Wash and dry the apples.
2. Remove the stalk, and then insert a wooden skewer into the hole.
3. Break the chocolate into pieces, and melt in a bowl set over a pan of simmering water.
4. Remove the chocolate from the heat, and dip in an apple up to about half way.
5. With the sprinkles in a small bowl, dip the apple into the sprinkles.
6. Stand sprinkle side down on a piece of grease proof paper and leave to set. Repeat with the remaining apples.

Popcorn cones

All you need to make these popcorn cones are some A4 sheets of coloured paper and a little sticky tape.

Holding your paper landscape, roll the bottom left corner around on itself. You want to start by aiming for the top right, then curving your roll down to the bottom right. Play around with the shape until you are happy with it, then secure with sticky tape. Fill with popcorn and enjoy!

BUNTING CAKE - Easy

You will need:
350g (12oz) butter or margarine
350g (12oz) caster sugar
6 medium eggs
350g (12oz) self raising flour

For decorating:
125g (5oz) butter or margarine
250g (10oz) sifted icing sugar
100g (4oz) red fondant
100g (4oz) blue fondant
thread, skewers and coloured paper

1. Preheat the oven to 180°c, 350°f, gas mark 4. Grease two 7 inch round cake tins, and line the bottom.

2. Cream the butter and sugar until light and fluffy. Beat in the eggs, and then gently fold in the flour.

3. Pour into the prepared tins, and bake for 40-45 minutes. The cake is fully cooked when a skewer inserted in the centre comes out clean.

4. To make the buttercream - cream the butter with the sifted icing sugar.

5. Once cool, use a cake cutting wire or bread knife to slice the top off each cake to give you a flat level surface.

6. Use a blob of buttercream to stick the cake to the board. Cover the top with a generous amount of buttercream, then add the 2nd cake, cut side down.

7. Cover the entire cake with a thin layer of buttercream. Refrigerate for at least 30 minutes. This will seal the cake and stop crumbs mixing in with the final finish.

8. Remove from the fridge and cover with the remaining buttercream. This can be done with a rough or smooth finish.

9. Thinly roll out the fondant. Using cutters, cut circles from the blue and small stars from the red. Stick the stars on the blue circles with a little edible glue or water, then place round the sides of the cake.

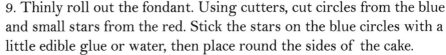

10. Cut diamond shapes out of the coloured paper, and glue around the thread by folding in half. Tie each end to the top of a skewer, and push these into the cake at a slight angle (you want the top to angle out more than the bottom).

11. The cake sparkler is optional, but it does add some 'wow'!

60

For the base:
250g (10oz) butter or margarine
250g (10oz) caster sugar
5 medium eggs
250g (10oz) self raising flour

For the tent:
50g (2oz) butter or margarine
50g (2oz) caster sugar
1 medium egg
50g (2oz) self raising flour

For decorating:
75g (3oz) butter or margarine
150g (6oz) sifted icing sugar
500g (20oz) blue fondant
200g (8oz) red fondant
200g (8oz) yellow fondant
optional: 3 paper straws, 3 skewers,
thread and coloured paper

1. Preheat the oven to 180°c, 350°f, gas mark 4.
Grease two 6 inch round cake tins, and line the bottom.

2. Cream the butter and sugar until light and fluffy. Beat in the eggs, and then gently fold in the flour.

3. Pour into the prepared tins, and bake for 40-45 minutes. The cake is fully cooked when a skewer inserted in the centre comes out clean.

4. To make the buttercream - cream the butter, gradually add the icing sugar, and cream together.

5. Using a cake cutting wire, or bread knife, slice the top off each cake to give you a flat level surface. Sandwich and cover with buttercream, then cover with blue fondant as shown on page 167.

6. Thinly roll out the red fondant. Make a triangle template out of paper (we did this 5cm wide x 6.5cm high) and use as a guide to cut the triangles.

7. Using a little edible glue or water, stick the triangles around the top of the cake.

8. Thinly roll out the yellow fondant. Cut with a small star cutter and stick on each triangle.

9. Roll pea sized balls with some of the yellow fondant and stick around the base of the cake.

Continued.....

Making the tent:

1. The tent cake is baked in an empty tin can. Make sure it is completely clean and dry, then grease and line the bottom. Make the cake as listed previously (pg62) and bake for 30-35 min.

2. Once cooled, cut the cake - about 1/3 down. With the smaller piece, shape into a cone by cutting away the corners in a circular motion around the cake. Sandwich back onto the base with buttercream, then cover the entire tent shape with a thin layer of buttercream.

3. Take a piece of blue fondant (you can add a little black food colouring to this if you wish to make it darker) roll thinly and cut a rectangle. Stick this to the tent trimming the top to fit.

4. Roll out the remaining red and yellow fondant, cut into strips. Stick these in an alternating pattern around the tent, trimming at the top where the roof starts. For the door - stick the tops of 2 of these strips to the blue/black fondant, pulling out the inner corners with your fingers.

5. For the roof strips, measure the height of the roof. Indent this distance on each strip of fondant. Cut from the dent up to the middle point of the top to create a long thin triangle shape. Below the dent, cut the corners to create a shallower triangle (see photo above).

6. Stick these to the roof of the tent, in an alternating pattern opposite to the walls (yellow tops red). Once complete, stick the tent to the main cake with a good blob of buttercream.

7. Create the bunting as on page 60, inserting the skewers into the paper straws 1st. Once tied, top each skewer with a small ball of yellow fondant.

Party bags

It wouldn't be a trip to the funfair without coming home with a goldfish in a bag - so why not recreate the fun (in a much more humane way) with these super cute soaps!

Take your time with these and only make one at a time as it can get a bit tricky. The soap can be melted again and again so don't worry if you make a mistake and it doesn't come out quite right. I would however recommend buying extra bags, as once the bags have had soap in you won't be able to use them again.

You will need:
150g (6oz) transparent melt and pour soap base per child
clear cello block bottom bags 95 x 165mm
plastic or rubber goldfish (before you start test in water whether they float or sink)
ribbon

Making a Goldfish in a bag soap

1. Cut the soap into small pieces. Place **half** in a microwave safe jug, and heat in 10 second bursts until melted. Alternatively place in a pan and melt slowly over a low heat.
Important: Do not overheat the soap.

2. Make sure your hands are clean of any soap residue before handling the bags. Carefully pour the soap into one of the bags - be careful not to get any soap on the sides. If you have a floaty fish add this to the bag now.

3. Leave to set for at least 30 minutes.

4. If you have a sinking fish, place the goldfish into the bag on top of the soap.

5. Melt the remaining soap as above and carefully pour on top of the fish. Once cool, tie the bag with ribbon.

Pirate Party

The invitation

Ahoy there matey! Set sail for an awesome party with these pirate scroll invitations.

You will need:
A4 paper
tea bags
ribbon
a candle

1. Soak the tea bag in half a cup of water, then rub over the paper, front and back.
2. Leave to dry, then cut in half along the width to give you A5 pieces.
3. Print or write the invitation on to the paper.
4. Light a candle, and carefully singe the edges all the way around.
5. Roll up the scroll and tie with ribbon. Voila!

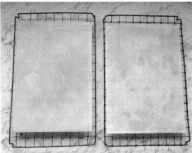

Setting the theme

This is a really popular theme that you can really go to town on. Have a go at making some of this fab pirate bunting out of wrapping paper and skull printouts. Cut the paper into large triangles allowing an extra 2cm tab at the top. Take a length of string and position the flags (make sure you leave some string bare at either end for tying). Fold the tab over the string and tape at the back.

The Games

~Pass the booty~

This is a variation of pass the parcel. All you need is a small bag to be the booty bag, some chocolate coins (enough for 1 per child) and some music. Sit the children in a circle and pass the booty bag while the music plays. When the music stops the child holding the booty takes a coin. You can finish the game once the bag is empty, or award a small prize for the next child to get the bag after all the coins are gone.

~Pirate boat fishing~

To play this you will need a fishing net and some small boats (see below). Place your boats in a paddling pool filled with water (inside use a large bowl) and take turns at trying to fish them out with the net. To make the boats as shown bottom right - tie 2 sticks together into a cross for a mast. Sew a small square of cotton to the horizontal stick. Take a cleaned out food container (such as a yoghurt or pâté pot) and put a ball of sticky tack in the centre of the bottom. Push the mast into this.

~Walk the plank~

Every pirate needs to have a plank aboard their ship! Create this fun balancing game simply with a plank of wood and 2 bricks. Can you make it across without falling to the sharks?

~Captain says~

Assign someone as 'captain' to shout the commands, such as 'Climb the rigging!', 'Scrub the decks!', 'Walk the plank!' etc. If they say 'Captain says' before the command everyone should act it out. But, if they just shout the command *without* saying 'Captain says' 1st, then anyone that does the action is out. The winner is the last player in.

~Buried treasure~

Fill a box with sand (or use the sandpit if you have one) then bury trinkets for the children to find. Provide trowels and plastic spades for the digging.

~Treasure hunt~

No pirate party is complete without a treasure hunt! As a great end of party game why not make it a hunt for the party bags. Use photos as the 'clues' for the next hiding place (even for the older of this age group not everyone will be reading) and lead everyone in a trail around the garden/room to find their 'treasure'.

Ahoy there matey! Here be buried treasure!

X

The Food

Well shiver me' timbers! A pirate banquet fit for the captain's table.
Little touches made to the presentation of the food really adds that 'wow' factor. Serve these tasty pirate treats along with your other party food for a fantastic pirate feast!

That little extra touch

So simple and really effective! Use these little extra touches to really set the table off.

• Fold some coloured paper in to little pirate boats to serve your crisps in.
• Hold your cheese and pineapple sticks together with sword cocktail sticks.
• Make pirates out of bananas by wrapping in a serviette and drawing on a pirate face.

Gingerbread Pirates

300g (10oz) self raising flour
3 tsp ground ginger
100g (4oz) sugar
50g (2oz) butter/margarine
3tbsp goldern syrup
4 tbsp milk

1. Preheat oven to 160°c, 325°f, gas mark 3.
2. Warm sugar, fat and syrup then add the dry ingredients.
3. Add milk & mix until firm.
4. Roll out & cut using a gingerbread man cutter.
5. Place onto a greased tray & bake for 10-15 minutes. Decorate with icing once cool.

Jelly boats

1 pack lemon or lime jelly
blue food colouring
oranges
cocktail sticks
jolly roger printouts
clear plastic cups

1. Make up the jelly according to the instructions.
2. Add a little blue colouring.
3. Pour into the plastic cups and chill in the fridge till set.
4. Cut the orange into half, and each half into 4.
5. Tape the flag to the stick, and push into the orange.

TREASURE CHEST *- Easy/moderate*

For the bottom cake:
175g (6oz) butter or margarine
175g (6oz) caster sugar
3 medium eggs
150g (5oz) self raising flour
25g (1oz) cocoa powder

For the top cake:
100g (4oz) butter or margarine
100g (4oz) caster sugar
2 medium eggs
75g (3oz) self raising flour
25g (1oz) cocoa powder

For decorating:
125g (5oz) butter or margarine
250g (10oz) sifted icing sugar
25g (1oz) cocoa powder
Chocolate coins & candy jewellery
4 crushed digestive biscuits
50g (2oz) orange fondant

1. Preheat the oven to 180°c, 350°f, gas mark 4. Grease two 6x4 inch loaf tins, and line the bottom.

2. Cream the butter and sugar until light and fluffy. Beat in the eggs, and then gently fold in the flour and cocoa.

3. Pour into the prepared tins, and bake for 60-65 minutes. The cake is fully cooked when a skewer inserted in the centre comes out clean.

4. To make the buttercream - cream the butter, gradually add the icing sugar, and cream together. Spread a thin layer over the cake board, then mix the cocoa powder into the remaining buttercream.

5. Using a bread knife, slice the top off each cake to give you a flat level surface. Place the bottom cake (the deeper one) in position on the board, and cover with buttercream. Arrange the coins on top, on the front half only, and score around the sides with a knife.

6. Take the top cake and turn upside down. Cut away the top corners to give you the curved lid shape. Cover with buttercream - leaving the ends free for lifting, then place on top of the base. Secure the cake by pushing in 3 cocktail sticks along the back through the lid and base (remember to remove these before serving!). Cover the holes left by the sticks, and the 2 lid ends with buttercream.

7. Thinly roll out the fondant, and cut into 2 long strips. Starting at the bottom, stick these onto the back of the chest, and up and over the lid. Trim to fit at the front, and indent with a piping nozzle to create 'rivets'.

8. Cover the board/buttercream base with the crushed biscuits.

Pirate Cake – For the experienced baker

For the base:
350g (12oz) butter or margarine
350g (12oz) caster sugar
6 medium eggs
350g (12oz) self raising flour

For the top:
100g (4oz) butter or margarine
100g (4oz) caster sugar
2 medium egg
100g (4oz) self raising flour

For decorating:
100g (4oz) butter or margarine
200g (8oz) sifted icing sugar
600g (24oz) white fondant
250g (10oz) red fondant
250g (10oz) black fondant

1. Preheat the oven to 180°c, 350°f, gas mark 4. Grease two 7 inch round cake tins, and line the bottoms.

2. Cream the butter and sugar until light and fluffy. Beat in the eggs, and then gently fold in the flour.

3. Pour into the prepared tins, and bake for 40-45 minutes. The cake is fully cooked when a skewer inserted in the centre comes out clean.

4. To make the buttercream - cream the butter, gradually add the icing sugar, and cream together.

5. Using a cake cutting wire, or bread knife, slice the top off each cake to give you a flat level surface. Sandwich and cover with buttercream, then cover with white fondant as shown on page 167.

6. Thinly roll out the red fondant, and cut into 3cm wide strips. You will need 12 strips.

7. Using a little edible glue or water, stick the red strips around the cake. Start from the bottom, gently pressing the strip onto the side of the cake and smoothing up and onto the top. For spacing - think of the cake as a clock face, start with the 12 and 6, and 3 and 9 positions 1st. Cut the strips where they meet on the top to leave a flat level surface.

8. To make the eye patch, 1st start by rolling out a little of the black fondant. Cut the patch to a size and shape you are happy with, and stick to the front of the cake.

9. Roll a long thin sausage out of black fondant. Roll flat, and cut to give it straight edges. Paint edible glue or water along the path you want the strap to follow, then carefully press the fondant

Continued.....

along this, joining at the back of the cake.

For the top cake:

1. Using two 5 inch cake tins, prepare the cake and tins as above and bake for 35-40 minutes.

2. Using a cake cutting wire, or bread knife, slice the top off each cake to give you a flat level surface. Sandwich and cover with buttercream, then cover with black fondant as shown on page 167.

3. Spread a desert spoonful of buttercream in the centre of the top of the base cake. Place the top cake on top of this.

4. Thinly roll out the remaining white fondant to cut the skull and cross bones from. You will find this easiest to do if you make a paper template 1st rather than trying to cut straight out.

5. Paint a little edible glue or water onto the back of the skull and bones, and stick into place on the top of the cake.

Optional: Finish off with a few randomly placed chocolate gold coins.

Party bags

Have these pirate loot bags as the prize at the end of the treasure hunt to make sure all your little pirates leave some with treasure.

As soon as you have your stencil they are very quick and simple to make (see below) and I'm sure you'll agree, they add the perfect finishing touch to your party.

Fill with:
• Chocolate coins
• Pirate transfer tattoos
• Eye patch
• Treasure map*

*Make these in the same way as the invitations on page 67, or print out on plain paper as colouring in sheets.

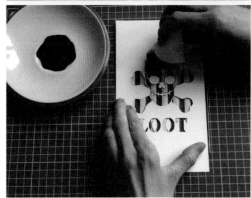

Making loot bags

You will need:
5 x 7 inch candy stripe bags
a 5 x 7 inch piece of cardboard
craft knife
black paint
sponge

1. Print or draw a skull and cross bones onto the piece of card. The template shown can be downloaded from **www.gemmadenham.com**.
2. Carefully cut out the design.
3. Place onto each bag in turn, and dab black paint over the stencil with the sponge.

Tip: You will get much better results if you only use a small amount of paint on the sponge at a time.

77

5 - 7 year olds

At this age children will have a lot more understanding and might be very eager and excited to help in the planning. They usually know what they want and how they want it, so talk through the themes and games with them, letting them pick out the things they like.

A few tips:

• The children have now started school so they will be used to being in big groups and will cope with a larger party size. Choose your number based on how many you feel comfortable entertaining, and the space you will be holding your party in.

• Children in this group will be able to play more organised games, although it is still important to allow a little 'free play'.

• The children will have a sense of fairness when it comes to winning and losing, so you can start naming winners for the games. That said, it is still a good idea to have a few 'everyone wins' type games.

• Not all parents will stay for the party, so you may want to check who is and who isn't so you don't end up with a room full to entertain by yourself! Don't be afraid to call on friends and family to help out. Unless your party is very small you'll need 2 to 3 adults.

• A party for a 5-7 year old usually lasts about 2 hours.

Monster Party

The invitation

Super simple to make and so much more fun than a standard invite!

Make these as cute or scary as you wish.

You will need:
A5 coloured paper (or some A4 cut in half)
White paper
Black pen
Glue
Scissors

  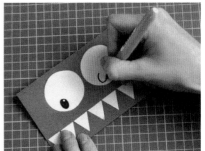

1. Fold the coloured paper up 5.5cm from the bottom, and fold the top down 6.5cm.
2. Cut circles and teeth from the white paper.
3. Glue into position and draw on eyes.
4. Print or write your invite in the centre section. Voila!

Setting the theme

Any Halloween decorations you have are perfect for this theme. How about making some of these spooky balloon ghosts?

1. Inflate some white balloons and tie.
2. Thread a needle with cotton, tying the other end to the end of the balloon.
3. Push the needle through the centre of a 50cm square piece of muslin. Remove the needle.
4. Draw on some eyes, and hang.

The Games

~Wrap the mummy~

Divide your little monsters into pairs, and give each pair a roll of toilet paper. Decide which person is the mummy, and which is the wrapper. The aim of the game is to be the 1st pair to fully wrap their mummy. Play this at least twice so everybody gets chance to be the mummy.

~Monster puzzle~

Print out or paint onto thick card 2 different coloured monsters. Cut each monster into 6 pieces, and hide the pieces around the room. Divide the children into 2 teams, and give them a colour to find (it is a good idea to have a photo or printout of the complete monster for the children to follow). The winning team is the 1st team to find and piece together their monster.

~Feed the monster~

All you need for this game is a large cardboard box, some paint and some bean bags. Draw a large monster head to fill one side of the box (make sure you give it a large open mouth). Cut out the mouth, then paint. Take turns at trying to throw a bean bag into the monsters mouth.

~Monster relay~

Divide your little monsters into 2 teams and line them up a one end of the room. At the other end of the room have 2 trick or treat buckets (or other suitable containers). In each bucket put small notes with monster commands such as 'Walk like a mummy', 'Stomp like Frankenstein' or 'Run like a spider' (make sure you have enough for each child). Played as a relay race, each player must run to the bucket, pick a command and then return to their team in the manor described. The 1st team to finish wins.

~Monster bowling~

You will need 6 washed out tin cans (make sure there are no sharp bits left on the opening) and some coloured paper. Create monster faces (see below) using the coloured paper cut into 10 x 24cm rectangles. Stick the faces around the cans, then stack into a pyramid. Take turns at trying to knock them all down with a tennis ball. After a few practice shots try setting the distance further away!

The Food

Satisfy all your little monsters with this spooktastic monster feast!
Put a little fun into sandwiches by turning them into monsters with cheese teeth and ham
tongues! Serve with these sweet treats and they'll be howling for more!

Monster Cupcakes

1. Preheat the oven to 190°c, gas mark 5.
2. Cream 100g butter with 100g sugar until light and fluffy. Beat in 2 eggs, and then gently fold in 100g flour and 25g cocoa.
3. Fill 12 paper cases with the mixture and bake for 15 mins.
4. To make the buttercream, cream 100g butter, gradually add 200g icing sugar and colouring, and cream together.
5. Pipe in a random pattern on top of each cake. Use chocolate buttons for eyes, and icing pens for the pupils and mouth.

Gruesome brew jellies

1 pack lime jelly
Candy teeth

1. Make up the jelly according to the instructions.
2. Once cool, leave in the fridge overnight to set.
3. Cut and mash the jelly up, then spoon into pots.
4. Arrange a few candy teeth on the top.

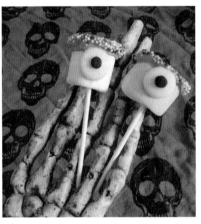

Marshmallow lollies

12 marshmallows
12 lolly sticks
Icing sugar
Food colouring
Sprinkles
White chocolate buttons
Black icing pen

1. Place 3 dessert spoons of icing sugar into a small bowl.
2. Mix slowly with the food colouring and a little cold water to form a thick paste.
3. Push a marshmallow onto a lolly stick and dip into the icing, then into the sprinkles.
4. Stick a chocolate button to the front and draw on a pupil.

Monster Cake - Easy

You will need:
200g (8oz) butter or margarine
200g (8oz) caster sugar
4 medium eggs
200g (8oz) self raising flour

For decorating:
175g (7oz) butter or margarine
350g (14oz) sifted icing sugar
blue food colouring
a little white and black fondant
(or you could use licorice rope and
giant white jazzies)

1. Preheat the oven to 180°c, 350°f, gas mark 4.
Grease two 6 inch round cake tins, and line the bottom.

2. Cream the butter and sugar until light and fluffy. Beat in the eggs, and then gently fold in the flour.

3. Pour into the prepared tins, and bake for 45-50 minutes. The cake is fully cooked when a skewer inserted in the centre comes out clean.

4. To make the buttercream - cream the butter, gradually add the icing sugar, and cream together. Add the food colouring and mix well.

5. Once cool, use a cake cutting wire or bread knife to slice the top off each cake to give you a flat level surface.

6. Use a blob of buttercream to stick the cake to the board. Cover the top with a generous amount of buttercream, then add the 2nd cake, cut side down.

7. Cover the entire cake with a thin layer of buttercream.

8. Fit a piping bag with a number 32 nozzle (large star shape), and cover the entire cake in piped rosettes. To pipe a rosette, pipe a little dollop in one place, push the bag down and draw up sharply to finish.

9. Thinly roll out the fondant. Cut a large circle from the white, and a small one from the black. Stick together with a little edible glue or water to make the eye, and place on the cake. Roll out the black into a long sausage, cut to size and place on the cake in an ark for the mouth.

Monster Cake — For the experienced baker

You will need:
250g (10oz) butter or margarine
250g (10oz) caster sugar
5 medium eggs
250g (10oz) self raising flour

For decorating:
75g (3oz) butter or margarine
150g (6oz) sifted icing sugar
250g (10oz) black fondant
250g (10oz) orange fondant
150g (8oz) green fondant
White chocolate buttons

1. Preheat the oven to 180°c, 350°f, gas mark 4. Grease two 6 inch round cake tins, and line the bottom.

2. Cream the butter and sugar until light and fluffy. Beat in the eggs, and then gently fold in the flour.

3. Place some of the mix into a paper cupcake case, and bake for 15-20 minutes. Pour the remainder into the prepared tins, and bake for 40-45 minutes. The cake is fully cooked when a skewer inserted in the centre comes out clean.

4. To make the buttercream - cream the butter, gradually add the sifted icing sugar, and cream together.

5. Using a cake cutting wire, or bread knife, slice the top off each cake to give you a flat level surface.

6. Use a blob of buttercream to stick the cake to the board. Cover the top with a generous amount of buttercream, then add the 2nd cake, cut side down.

7. Cover the entire cake with a thin layer of buttercream.

8. Knead the black fondant until pliable. Roll out into a long rectangle (long enough to go around the cake). Measure the height of the cake and cut to size.

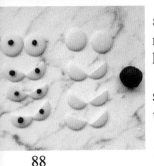

9. Carefully wrap the black around the cake, trimming at the back to fit.

10. Knead the orange fondant until pliable, and roll out to a

Continued.....

thickness of about 5mm. Using the cake tin as a guide, cut a splat shape larger than the tin. Place on top of the cake, and smooth down. Use edible glue or water under the 'drips' to stick these to the sides of the cake.

11. Take the chocolate buttons, and using the edible glue, stick small balls of black onto them to make eyes. Cut some of the buttons in half to give you a different shape. Stick these around the sides of the cake.

12. Remove the cupcake from the paper case, and cover with a thin layer of buttercream.

13. Thinly roll out the green fondant and cover the cup cake. This is the monster body.

14. With the green, roll 4 long sausage shapes. Flatten the end of each with your fingers, and make 2 cuts to create 3 fingers/toes on each. Round and shape these with your fingers.

15. Take the 2 legs, and flatten the top. Apply a little edible glue or water to the underside, and stick to the top of the cake so that they hang down the front.

16. Spread a little buttercream to the bottom of the cupcake, and place on top of the legs.

17. With your fingers or a round fondant tool, create hollows to fit the eyes into and stick these into place.

18. Create a mouth by cutting a slit with a knife, and stick the arms onto the sides.

Party bags

How creepy are these monster hand party bags? And how perfect for your monster party!

Super quick and easy to make, and the kids will love them!

You will need:
Clear disposable vinyl gloves
Black ribbon
Sweets
Plastic spiders (optional)

This couldn't be an easier make! Simply fill each glove with sweets (making sure you get right down into each finger), and tie the end securely with ribbon. If using the spiders, glue to the top of the glove with a blob of PVA glue and leave to dry.

Traditional bags

Want to go for a more traditional party bag? Then fill your chosen party bag with spooky dressing up accessories such as:

• Masks
• Fangs
• Claws/fingers
• Face paints
• Fake scars/wounds

Add a handful of sweets and a piece of the all important birthday cake, and you're all done.

As an alternative to the plastic party bag, try colourful paper bags - you can always print or stamp these with any design or text of your choosing.

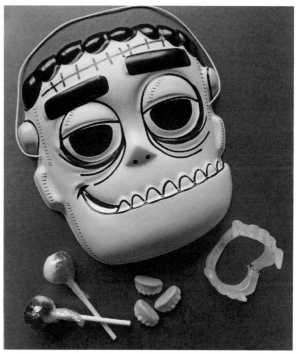

SPORTS PARTY

On the invitation:

Please come to
Jack's Sports Party
On Saturday 6th July
2-4pm
On the village green

R.S.V.P 01234567891

On the hand:

You're invited!

The invitation

Set the theme as you mean to go on with these giant hand invitations. You will find a template for these to download at **www.gemmadenham.com**. Simply print onto some coloured card, cut to size, then write your invitation onto the back.

Good with computers, type and print the invitation details onto the back of the hands before cutting.

Setting the theme

Have plenty of sports equipment out for the children to play with while you wait for all the guests to arrive. Football, basketball, tennis, and cricket bats will all keep them entertained whilst you get everything set up.

The Games

This party is not really suitable for in the home, but perfect for the garden or park.
Use a village hall if the weather or time of year isn't right.

~Assault Course~

This is a great team game. Set up an assault course using cones to run or dribble a football round, play tunnels to crawl through, tennis balls to bounce with a racket etc. Spilt your party into 2 teams, and after a practise go, time each team completing the course in a relay fashion. The fastest team wins.

~Discus throw~

Have a flag or sign as the starting point and see how far you can throw the discus (frisbee).

~High jump~

The high jump always proves to be a great laugh and gets very competitive.
To make the high jump as shown right, take 2 pieces of wood about 1 meter in length. Screw each of these to large block (this will give them the weight and stability to stand). Drill holes all the way up your stands, about 2 inches apart. Hammer a wooden dowel in each hole. Paint if desired, and use a garden cane as the cross beam.

~Scooter Race~

Your space will decide how many can race at a time. Set a start and finish line and off you go!

~100 Meter sprint~

(or however long your garden is!)
For a small party you can do this as one big race. For larger parties split into 2 teams and do relay style.

~Long jump~

Stick some masking tape to the floor as a starting line and see who can jump the furthest.

~Foam hand craft~

Blank foam hands can be bought from craft providers, or easily made from foam sheets. Allow 1 per child and provide pens for them to make their own design. A great activity and take home item that they can use during the party to cheer on their team.

The Food

Calling all sports fans! These mouth-watering concession stand food ideas will settle the cravings of your little athletes. Hot dogs and team burgers served with chips and dip, with sports cookies for afters. What more could you ask for!

Sports Cookies

225g (8oz) butter or margarine
110g (4oz) sugar
275g (10oz) plain flour
Fondant icing

1. Preheat the oven to 180°c, 350°f, gas mark 4.
2. Cream the butter and sugar until light and fluffy.
3. Sift in the flour, and mix to form a firm dough.
4. Roll out and cut with a circular cutter.
5. Bake for 15 minutes.
6. Once cool, decorate with the icing balls as shown on page 102.

Team burgers

Get into the team spirit and give your burgers that little something extra with these team flags.

All you need are:
Cocktail sticks and paper

Each mini flag wants to be about 3 x 5cm.
1. Find and print out your chosen design - this could be the badge of the team you support, or just something generic and supportive like the ones shown.
2. Cut out the flags, and stick to the top of cocktail sticks with a little tape.
3. Once your burgers are ready, stick a flag into the top and serve.

BANNER CAKE - Easy

You will need:

350g (12oz) butter or margarine
350g (12oz) caster sugar
6 medium eggs
350g (12oz) self raising flour

For decorating:

125g (5oz) butter or margarine
250g (10oz) sifted icing sugar
100g (4oz) red fondant
100g (4oz) blue fondant
100g (4oz) yellow fondant
thread, skewers and paper

1. Preheat the oven to 180°c, 350°f, gas mark 4. Grease two 7 inch round cake tins, and line the bottom.

2. Cream the butter and sugar until light and fluffy. Beat in the eggs, and then gently fold in the flour.

3. Pour into the prepared tins, and bake for 45-50 minutes. The cake is fully cooked when a skewer inserted in the centre comes out clean.

4. To make the buttercream - cream the butter, gradually add the icing sugar, and cream together.

5. Once cool, use a cake cutting wire or bread knife to slice the top off each cake to give you a flat level surface.

6. Use a blob of buttercream to stick the cake to the board. Cover the top with a generous amount of buttercream, then add the 2nd cake, cut side down.

7. Cover the entire cake with a thin layer of buttercream. Refrigerate for at least 30 minutes. This will seal the cake and stop crumbs mixing in with the final finish.

8. Remove from the fridge and cover with the remaining buttercream. This can be done with a rough or smooth finish.

9. Roll the fondant into marble sized balls, and place around the base of the cake.

10. Tie a 10 x 5cm banner* to the top of the skewers, and push these into the cake at a slight angle (you want the top to angle out more than the bottom).

*You can make any banner of your choosing. The one shown can be downloaded from www.gemmadenham.com.

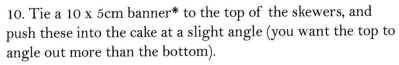

SPORTS CAKE *– for the experienced baker*

You will need:
200g (8oz) butter or margarine
200g (8oz) caster sugar
4 medium eggs
200g (8oz) self raising flour
25g (1oz) cocoa powder

For decorating:
35g (2oz) chocolate sprinkles
Chocolate buttercream:
75g (3oz) butter or margarine
125g (5oz) sifted icing sugar
25g (1oz) cocoa powder
Green buttercream:
50g (2oz) butter or margarine
100g (4oz) sifted icing sugar
Green food colouring

1. Preheat the oven to 180°c, 350°f, gas mark 4.
Grease two 6 inch round cake tins, and line the bottom.

2. Cream the butter and sugar until light and fluffy. Beat in the eggs, and then gently fold in the flour and cocoa.

3. Pour into the prepared tins, and bake for 40-45 minutes. The cake is fully cooked when a skewer inserted in the centre comes out clean.

4. To make the chocolate buttercream - cream the butter, gradually add the icing sugar and cocoa, and cream together.

5. Using a cake cutting wire, or bread knife, slice the top off each cake to give you a flat level surface. Cover with a generous amount of buttercream, then add the 2nd cake, cut side down.

6. Cover the sides of the cake with chocolate buttercream. Pour the chocolate sprinkles onto a plate, and roll the cake in the sprinkles. Make sure you cover all the side, all the way around.

7. To make the green buttercream - cream the butter, gradually add the icing sugar, and cream together. Add the green food colouring, and mix well.

8. Spread a thin layer of buttercream over the top of the cake. Be careful not to mix this with the sides.

9. Fit a piping bag with a no.233 piping nozzle (grass/hair nozzle), and fill with the buttercream. Starting around the edges and working in- squeeze, pull and release the icing bag to create the grass effect.

Continued.....

Baseball:
Thinly roll out white fondant, and cut with a circle cutter. Using the cutter, indent the fondant at the sides to give you a guide to follow. Roll red fondant into thin strings, and stick along the guide. Add smaller pieces of this for stitching.

Basket ball:
Thinly roll out orange fondant, and cut with a circle cutter. Lightly press with a sieve to give the textured effect. Roll black fondant into thin stings and stick in the pattern shown above.

Football:
Thinly roll out white fondant, and cut with a circle cutter. Roll out black fondant and cut into small pentagons. Stick one to the centre of the circle, and indent the above pattern with a blunt knife. Stick the remaining pentagons around the edges trimming where necessary.

Rugby ball:
Thinly roll out brown fondant, and cut with a circle cutter. Using a cocktail stick, indent a line down the centre of the circle, then 4 holes on either side of this. Cut thin stripes of white fondant, and stick as shown below.

Tennis ball:
Thinly roll out green fondant, and cut with a circle cutter. Roll white fondant into a thin string, and stick in a loop shape to the circle.

Cricket ball:
Thinly roll out red fondant, and cut with a circle cutter. Using the cutter, indent the fondant as shown. Roll white fondant into thin strings, cut into rice sized pieces, and stick as stitching.

 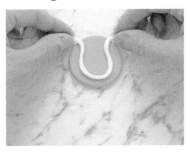 

Party bags

Keep the party going (and everyone active) with these sport inspired party bags!

Using a drawstring bag as your base, fill with sporting goods such as:

• Frisbee
• Tennis ball
• Whistle
• Medal (see below for how to make yummy chocolate ones!)
• Sweat bands
• Skipping rope
• Drinks bottle
• Shuttlecock
• Ping pong ball

Pick a couple of items and add a few sweets and piece of the birthday cake.

Making medals

You will need:
80cm of ribbon per medal
Foil wrapped chocolate coins

Simply cut the ribbon to length. Bring the 2 cut ends together, and attach a gold coin with a blob of PVA glue. Leave to dry, and there you have it!

Chocolate Party

The invitation

Impressive, elegant, and very simple to make. You will find this 'Golden ticket' design available to download at **www.gemmadenham.com**. Type your invitation details onto the design, and print onto some gold card. Cut to size and *voila!*

Setting the theme

Watch everyone's eyes light up at this chocolate tree! A definite show stopper of a centre piece for any table.
'Plant' a small branch in a plant pot, and hang with wrapped chocolates - yum!

The Games

This party goes down well with kids of all ages, after all, who doesn't like chocolate! This could easily go in the older 8-10 age group, but I wouldn't go younger than this group because of the fine motor skills needed for some of the games.

~The flour game~

This game is so much fun, and one no-one minds losing!
Fill a teacup with flour. Upturn this onto a tray (to create a little flour castle), and place a chocolate on top. Using a table knife, take turns at cutting away a slice of the flour *without* the chocolate falling! The person who makes the chocolate fall has to eat it by retrieving it using only their mouths! Reset and play again with the remaining players until there is only 1 person left - the winner!

~Make your own chocolate lolly~

Provide everyone with a sheet of grease proof paper (write names on so you know who's is who's at the end), and a lolly stick. Melt some chocolate, and pour into disposable piping bags. Let the children pipe their own lollies onto the sticks, and decorate with sprinkles and mini marshmallows. Chill to set in the fridge, and give out at the end.

~Chopstick chocolates~

Give each child a small bowl of round chocolates (such as malteasers), an empty paper cup and a pair of chopsticks. The aim is to be the fastest to move your chocolates from the bowl, into the cup, using only the chopsticks.

~Button head~

This game is hilarious and all you need is a packet of chocolate buttons!
Give each child 1 chocolate button. The aim is to get the button from your forehead - into your mouth, without touching it! The winner is the 1st person to achieve it.

~Chocolate wrap~

Wrap a bar of chocolate in multiple layers of wrapping paper. Wearing gloves, you have 10 seconds to unwrap as many layers as you can, then pass it on. The child that unwraps the last layer wins the chocolate.

The Food

You can't have a chocolate party without a chocolate fountain! Both impressive and tasty, have it as your centre piece and serve with all the normal party food. Provide fruit and marshmallows for dipping.

Chocolate Cupcakes

You will need:
100g (4oz) butter
100g (4oz) caster sugar
2 medium eggs
100g (4oz) self raising flour
25g (1oz) cocoa powder

For decorating:
100g (4oz) butter
200g (8oz) icing sugar
Lemon or vanilla essence
Chocolates of your choice

1. Preheat the oven to 190°c, gas mark 5.
2. Cream the butter and sugar until light and fluffy. Beat in the eggs, and then gently fold in the flour and cocoa.
3. Fill 12 paper cases with the mixture and bake for about 15 minutes.
4. To make the buttercream, cream the butter, gradually add the icing sugar and flavouring, and cream together.
5. Fit a piping bag with a large star nozzle, and fill with the buttercream. Pipe a swirl on top of each cake (start from the outside working in with a spiral).
6. Top with a chocolate.

Party bags and prizes

Why not set up a sweet shop as a prize station. Just fill empty jars with chocolates and sweets. Then, everytime someone wins a game, they can come and help themselves to one item from the shop.

Provide some paper candy bags, and the sweet shop doubles up for party bags. At the end of the party let the children fill a bag to take home.

109

Anti-gravity cake – *Easy/moderate*

You will need:
200g (8oz) butter or margarine
200g (8oz) caster sugar
4 medium eggs
200g (8oz) self raising flour
25g (1oz) cocoa powder

For decorating:
50g (2oz) butter or margarine
100g (4oz) sifted icing sugar
25g (1oz) cocoa powder
50g (2oz) milk chocolate
3 packets chocolate fingers
1 large bag sugar coated candies
1 sweet bag, 1 skewer and 1 straw

For an easier version of this cake miss out steps 7 & 8 and have the cake without the anti-gravity part.

1. Preheat the oven to 180°c, 350°f, gas mark 4. Grease two 6 inch round cake tins, and line the bottom.

2. Cream the butter and sugar until light and fluffy. Beat in the eggs, and then gently fold in the flour and cocoa.

3. Pour into the prepared tins, and bake for 40-45 minutes. The cake is fully cooked when a skewer inserted in the centre comes out clean.

4. To make the chocolate buttercream - cream the butter, gradually add the icing sugar and cocoa, and cream together.

5. Using a cake cutting wire, or bread knife, slice the top off each cake to give you a flat level surface. Cover with a generous amount of buttercream, then add the 2nd cake, cut side down.

6. Cover the entire cake in buttercream, then stick the chocolate fingers around the sides.

7. Push the skewer all the way into the cake at an angle. Cover with the straw.

8. Melt the milk chocolate in a bowl over a pan of simmering water. Off heat, spread a little onto a candy, and stick to the base of the straw. Continue working upwards until the straw is covered.

9. Pour the remaining candies onto the top of the cake. Carefully position the sweet bag on top of the straw, and tie the cake with a ribbon.

The invitation

Call your soldiers for duty with these army themed invitations. Complete with bullet holes and mud splatters, what little soldier could resist!

You will find the template for this army invitation ready to download from **www.gemmadenham.com**. Simply type (or write) on your details, and print on good quality paper. Voila!

Setting the theme

• Print out targets and pin to fences or sticky tack them around the room.
• Hang parachuting army men by threading some cotton through the centre of the parachute.
• Stencil empty boxes with army themed words and stack around the room.

The Games

All of these games are best played in teams. When the guests arrive, how about assigning them a coloured sash - have 2 different colours and this will be their team for the party.

~Assault course~

An integral part of any soldiers training. Create an assault course with tyres to run through (talk to your local garage or scrap yard), a tunnel to crawl through, a balance beam (we used the 'legs' from old pallets), and a camo net to commando crawl under. Let your soldiers practice, then time how long it takes each team to complete it.

~Target practice~

Set up 12 washed out tin cans (make sure there are no sharp bits left on the opening) into 2 pyramids - one for each team, and see who can 'shoot' them all down the fastest. Use foam/cork bullet shooting toy guns if you have them, or alternatively 'bomb' your target with tennis balls.

~Tug of war~

An old favourite. Have the teams line up at each end of a rope, and take hold. Each team pulls at the rope, and the winners are the team to pull the other team over the central line.

~Water balloon battle~

Arm each team with a bucket of filled water balloons. Create or name a safe place (or base) for each team, and let battle commence.

~Rescue mission~

All you will need for this game are some small plastic soldiers. Hide the soldiers around the room/garden, and assign each team a colour to find. The 1st team to find and rescue all their men (or the team to find the most in 5 minutes) are the winners.

~Bomb pinata~

Allow one pinata per team and race to see who can be the 1st to 'explode' their bomb. Detailed instructions on how to make this are on page 166.

~Scavenger hunt~

Give the teams a list of items. Hide the items (unless naturally occurring), and have the players search for them. The 1st team to find everything on the list wins.

SCAVENGER HUNT

- ARMY FIGURE
- PINE CONE
- BROWN LEAF
- AN INSECT
- A STICK
- SOMETHING ROUND
- SOMETHING POINTY
- SOMETHING YOU CAN EAT

The Food

Send your hungry soldiers running for the mess table with this half time battle banquet! A hot meal of hot dogs and beans, finished off with a soldier cupcake.

Soldier Cupcakes

You will need:
100g (4oz) butter
100g (4oz) caster sugar
2 medium eggs
100g (4oz) self raising flour
25g (1oz) cocoa powder

For decorating:
75g (3oz) butter
150g (6oz) icing sugar
Green food colouring
Plastic soldiers

1. Preheat the oven to 190°c, gas mark 5.
2. Cream the butter and sugar until light and fluffy. Beat in the eggs, and then gently fold in the flour and cocoa.
3. Fill 12 paper cases with the mixture and bake for about 15 minutes.
4. To make the buttercream, cream the butter, gradually add the icing sugar and colouring, and cream together.
5. Fit a piping bag with a no.233 piping nozzle (grass/hair nozzle), and fill with the buttercream. Squeeze, pull and release the icing bag to create the grass effect. Top with a soldier.

That little extra touch

So simple and really effective! Use these little extra touches to really set the table off.

• Replace the labels on drinks bottles with something a little more in theme - like these camoflarge H2O designs.

• The army theme is very 'no fuss' so set out your cutlery in an empty tin can.

• Mess tins, metal trays and enamel plates are the perfect way to serve and set off the food.

SOLDIER CAKE - Easy

You will need:
200g (8oz) butter or margarine
200g (8oz) caster sugar
4 medium eggs
175g (7oz) self raising flour
25g (2oz) cocoa powder

For decorating:
125g (5oz) butter or margarine
250g (10oz) sifted icing sugar
50g (2oz) cocoa powder
green food colouring
2 crushed digestive biscuits

1. Preheat the oven to 180°c, 350°f, gas mark 4. Grease two 6 inch round cake tins, and line the bottom.

2. Cream the butter and sugar until light and fluffy. Beat in the eggs, and then gently fold in the flour and cocoa.

3. Pour into the prepared tins, and bake for 40-45 minutes. The cake is fully cooked when a skewer inserted in the centre comes out clean.

4. To make the chocolate buttercream - cream 75g (3oz) butter with 150g (6oz) sifted icing sugar and the cocoa.

5. Using a cake cutting wire, or bread knife, slice the top off each cake to give you a level surface

6. Use a blob of chocolate buttercream to stick the cake to the board. Cover the top with buttercream, then add the 2nd cake, cut side down. Cover the sides of the cake with the remaining buttercream. Spread a little in a random pattern on the top of the cake.

7. Hold a fork against the side of the cake. Keeping the fork steady, slowly rotate the cake to leave running indentations around the entire cake. Repeat further up until the whole side of the cake is covered all the way around.

8. To make the green buttercream - cream 50g (2oz) butter with 100g (4oz) sifted icing sugar and the green food colouring. Fit a piping bag with a no.233 piping nozzle (grass/hair nozzle), and fill with the buttercream.

9. Squeeze, pull and release the icing bag to create the grass effect around the chocolate buttercream. Arrange plastic soldiers on the top, then cover their bases with crushed biscuits. Continue this around the base of the cake.

TANK CAKE – For the experienced baker

For the main body:
350g (12oz) butter or margarine
350g (12oz) caster sugar
6 medium eggs
350g (12oz) self raising flour
25g (1oz) cocoa powder

For the gun turret:
50g (2oz) butter or margarine
50g (2oz) caster sugar
1 medium egg
25g (1oz) self raising flour
25g (1oz) cocoa powder

For decorating:
200g (8oz) icing sugar
100g (4oz) butter/margarine
600g (24oz) green fondant
150g (6oz) black fondant

1. Preheat the oven to 180°c, 350°f, gas mark 4.
Grease two 7.5 x 10 inch rectangular (or roasting tins).

2. Cream the butter and sugar until light and fluffy. Beat in the eggs, and then gently fold in the flour and cocoa.

3. Pour into the prepared tins, and bake for 40-45 minutes. The cake is fully cooked when a skewer inserted in the centre comes out clean.

4. To make the chocolate buttercream - cream the butter, gradually add the icing sugar and cocoa, and cream together. Sandwich the 2 layers of cake together with buttercream.

5. Using a bread knife, cut the 2 long sides off the cake to give a flush edge. Then, cut one of the shorter sides (to be the front) downwards at an angle as shown above.

6. Cover the entire cake with a thin layer of buttercream. Roll the black fondant out thinly, then cut and cover the 2 long sides of the cake.

7. Keeping 50g of black aside, knead the black and green fondant together to mix. Roll this thinly, then cut a long rectangle the width of the cake. Cover the top and ends of the cake. Keep the remainder sealed in a bag for later on.

8. Roll out the black, and cut into a long strip about 2cm wide. Indent this as shown left to make the caterpillar tracks.

9. Paint a little water or edible glue along the base of the black sides, and up each end. Push the tread onto this, and cut each end to taper into the top.

120
Continued.....

10. Making more if you have to or using off cuts - stick tread to the front and back of the tank at each side.

11. Make wheels by stamping out and indenting circles using piping nozzles (shown above), and stick to the sides of the tank. You will need 7 per side.

12. Roll out the green fondant mix, and cut into long strips 7cm wide. Stick these to the top of the cake so that they fold down onto the sides, and partially down the front and back.

13. Make the gun turret in a 4-5 inch tin using the previous method. Bake for 20 - 25 minutes.

14. Once cool, cut the top off the cake to give you a flat level surface. Cut 2 of the sides off as shown below and cover with buttercream and the green mix fondant. Stick the turret to the top of the tank with a blob of buttercream.

You should now have the basic tank shape - all that's left is to add the details:

- Roll out the green fondant mix and cut into small rectangles. Stick these along the corner strips, on the top and sides.

- Use piping nozzles to indent different sized circles.

- Use a cocktail stick to indent rows of 'rivets'

- 'Paint' on mud using a dry food brush and cocoa powder.

  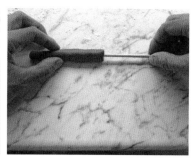 

Making the gun:

1. Roll a long thin sausage shape with the green mix fondant, and push a skewer through the centre until it pokes out about 5mm.

2. Add a ball of black fondant to the end, and push into shape.

3. Cut 2 thin strips of green fondant. Stick 1 around the join, and the other around the base. Push the finished gun into the gun turret.

Party bags

Simple is more with an army theme, so these brown paper bags are perfect! Leave as they are, or stick on a themed design or thank you message such as the one shown left. This design can be downloaded from **www.gemmadenham.com**.

Fill your party bags with army related things such as:

- Plastic soldiers
- Dog tags
- Chocolate medals (see page 103)
- Water balloons (empty!)
- Flying polystyrene glider
- Parachuting soldiers

And don't forget a wrapped piece of the yummy birthday cake!

DANCE PARTY

The invitation

Invite your honoured guests in style with these VIP passes, and watch the look of excitement as they receive one.

You will find the template for these VIP pass invitations ready to download from **www.gemmadenham.com**. Simply type (or write) on your details, and print on photo glossy paper.

Voila!

Setting the theme

Disco Lights can be bought fairly cheaply and will make a huge difference to your party.

Have plenty of dressing up accessories on hand such as glow sticks, glasses, wigs and gloves. You will find they become a game all by themselves!

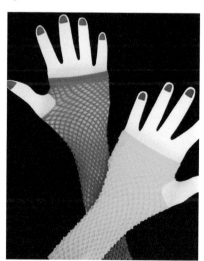

The Games

This is a great indoor party, though you will need to be able to clear a room,
or hire a small village hall depending on your space.

~Style Station~

Set out some dress up accessories like feather boa's, necklaces, sunglasses etc.
and have an area where you can spray the dancers hair with glitter or neon colours.

~Limbo~

Use a broom handle or feather boa as the limbo stick. Two people hold each end of the stick
horizontally in the air, and the dancers line up behind. Everyone in line must go under the stick
by walking forwards whilst bending backward under the stick. If someone touches the stick or
falls they are out. Those who succeed go into the next round and the stick is lowered.
Continue lowering the stick until there is only one player left.

~Dance Competition~

Get the music going and hold a dance competition! Award prizes for most creative dance, best
dance move, most improved dancer etc. You could also set a group challenge and get each team
to choreograph their own routine.

~New moves~

Time to learn some crazy dance song moves! Get a music video up on the tv to follow and learn
the moves to. You wants songs such as The Macarena, The Ketchup song and Gangnam style.

~Dance off!~

Have a games console or a friend that is happy to lend you one? Pop on a dance game and have a
dance off!

~Freeze frame~

Set the music going and assign someone as the caller. As everyone dances, the caller shouts out
a word for the dancers to respond to:
• Fast Forward: Dance really, really fast!
• Slow Motion: Slow it right down.
•Stop: Dancers have to immediately stop and stand still.
•Pause: Immediately stop but holding the pose - like you would in musical statues.
•Eject: Jump in the air and sit down.

The Food

Go dance crazy with these fabulous sweet treats to serve alongside your savouries.
Have plenty of colourful cordial, and water bottles on hand for rehydrating!

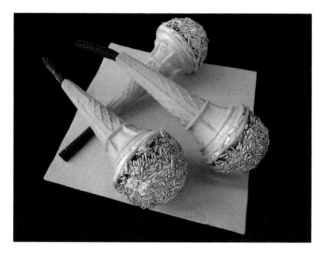

Microphone cakes – Makes 6

1. Preheat the oven to 180°c, gas mark 4.
2. Cream 100g butter with 100g sugar until light and fluffy. Beat in 2 eggs, and then gently fold 100g self raising flour and 25g cocoa powder in.
3. Pour into a greased 6 inch tin, and bake for 40-45 minutes.
5. Once cool, crumb the cake into a bowl.
6. A little at a time, add 100g of chocolate buttercream whilst mixing, until the mix will form a dough.
7. Divide the mixture into 6 and roll into balls.
8. Melt 100g milk chocolate. Dip in the top of an icecream cone, and push a ball onto it. Repeat with the remaining 5. Chill till set.
9. Spread the ball of each cone with chocolate, and dip into a cup of chocolate sprinkles.
10. Spray with edible silver shimmer spray, and stand in a glass for support till dry.

Star biscuits

225g (8oz) butter
110g (4oz) sugar
275g (10oz) plain flour
Fondant icing

1. Preheat the oven to 180°c, 350°f, gas mark 4.
2. Cream the butter and sugar until light and fluffy.
3. Sift in the flour, and mix to form a firm dough.
4. Roll out on a floured surface and cut with a large star cutter.
5. Place on a greased baking tray, and bake for 15 minutes.
6. Once cool, decorate with fondant, spray with edible shimmer spray, or stamp with fondant letter stamps.

DISCO CAKE *- Easy/moderate*

You will need:
200g (8oz) butter or margarine
200g (8oz) caster sugar
4 medium eggs
200g (8oz) self raising flour

For decorating:
50g (2oz) butter/margarine
100g (4oz) icing sugar
500g (20oz) black fondant
50g (2oz) yellow fondant
50g (2oz) pink fondant
50g (2oz) turquoise fondant
Glitter ball bauble

For an easier version of this cake, cover with buttercream instead of the black fondant- use double the amount of buttercream as listed below, and mix in some food colouring of your choice.

1. Preheat the oven to 180°c, 350°f, gas mark 4.
Grease two 6 inch round cake tins, and line the bottom.

2. Cream the butter and sugar until light and fluffy. Beat in the eggs, and then gently fold in the flour.

3. Pour into the prepared tins, and bake for 40-45 minutes. The cake is fully cooked when a skewer inserted in the centre comes out clean.

4. To make the buttercream - cream the butter, gradually add the icing sugar, and cream together.

5. Using a cake cutting wire, or bread knife, slice the top off each cake to give you a level surface

6. Use a blob of buttercream to stick the cake to the board. Cover the top with a generous amount of buttercream, then add the 2nd cake, cut side down. Cover the cake with a thin layer of buttercream and cover with the black fondant as shown on page 167.

7. Thinly roll out the yellow, pink and turquoise fondant. Cut into strips about 3cm wide.

8. Cut the top of each strip into a point by removing the corners to about 1/3 down (as above).

9. Stick to the cake with a little edible glue or water, trimming at the bottom to fit.

10. Roll some of the black fondant into a donut shape and stick in the centre of the top of the cake. Sit the glitter ball onto this.

Party bags

Keep the party going with these fun mp3 player party bags!

Create these party bags simply, by printing out and sticking 'screens' and 'controls' onto neon coloured tall paper party bags. The sound bar and controls can be downloaded from **www.gemmadenham.com**.

Fill your party bags with dance related things such as:

• Glow sticks
• Hair bands
• Glow in the dark accessories
• Colourful/swirly lollies
• Whistles

Don't forget a wrapped piece of the yummy birthday cake!

Sweet cones

Another idea that works well for a dance party bag is a sweet cone. Fill clear coloured cellophane cone bags with an assortment of colourful sweets, and tie the end with a ribbon.

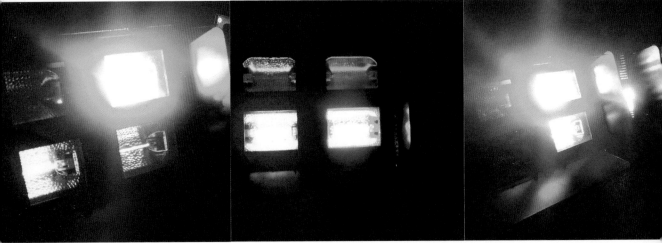

8 - 10 year olds

The invitation

Set the theme as you mean to go on with these movie ticket invitations. You will find the template for these to download at **www.gemmadenham.com**. Simply type (or write) your invitation details onto the front, and print out on some thin card.

The Party

This is a great party for kids who want to feel a bit more grown up and have a less childish party. It is also a nice stress free one from a parents perspective!

Make sure the film is age appropriate, and include the title on the invites to inform the parents.

The Games

A movie party can be as simple as everyone sitting watching the film with some popcorn. If you do want to play a few games before the film starts, then have a go at these.

~Suckers~

Each player has a bowl of small sweets or chocolates (make sure each player has the same number), a straw, and a paper cup. They must race to move all the chocolates from the bowl into the cup - using just the straw! 1st player to finish wins.

~Who am I?~

Everyone secretly writes down the name of a character from a film onto a sticky note. Pass this to the person sat next to you, who without looking at it, sticks it to their forehead. The idea is to ask a series of questions to determine who you are, but the questions should only be answered by "Yes" or "No". Such as, 'Am I a cartoon', 'Am I an animal', 'Am I a superhero'. Continue until the character is guessed, then move on to the next player.

~Sorting Skills~

Each player has a bowl of coloured candies (the same number for each player), and a row of cups/pots (You will need a different pot for each different colour of sweet you have.) The object of the game is to separate your sweets into colours by moving 1 at a time in the fastest time. Only 1 hand can be used so put the other behind your back! Play this game 2 at a time unless you have a lot of pots!

~Over under~

Divide your guests into 2 teams and line them up. The player at the front starts with the balloon and passes it over their head to the next player - they then pass the balloon on by passing it through their legs. Continue passing the balloon down the line alternating between over the head and through the legs until you get to the end of the line. The last player runs with the balloon to the front of the line and play continues until the original front player is back at the font. 1st team to complete the whole cycle wins.

For an alternative this game can also be played with knees and elbows. Hold the balloon between your knees and pass onto the next player who takes it with their knees. Conquered that? Then try passing with your elbows. For a really tricky one try passing down the line elbow to knee!

The Food

These mouth-watering movie snack ideas come straight from the concession stand. Hot dogs and pizza served with nachos and popcorn. What more could you ask for!

Child friendly nacho recipes

Lightly spiced

175g (7oz) packet plain tortilla chips
400g (12oz) tin chopped tomatoes, strained
1 cup sweetcorn
400g (12oz) tin kidney beans, strained
½ teaspoon ground cumin
1 teaspoon paprika
2 rashes bacon, rind removed and diced
100g (4oz) grated cheddar cheese

1. Cook the diced bacon and set to one side.
2. In a large bowl, add the tomatoes and crush to make a lumpy sauce.
3. Add the corn, beans, cumin, paprika and bacon and give the mixture a good stir.
4. With a slotted spoon, place the mixture on top of the chips, then sprinkle with cheese.
5. Place under a hot grill for 4–5 minutes to melt the cheese.

Creamy cheese

175g (7oz) packet plain tortilla chips
1 carton sour cream
100g (4oz) grated cheddar cheese

1. Tip the tortilla chips into an oven proof dish, and drizzle with sour cream.
2. Sprinkle the cheese over the top.
3. Place under a hot grill for 3-4 minutes.

Cheesy salsa

175g (7oz) packet plain tortilla chips
225g (9oz) jar salsa
100g (4oz) cheddar cheese

1. Tip the tortilla chips into an oven proof dish, and pour over the salsa.
2. Grate the cheddar cheese, and sprinkle over the top.
3. Place under a hot grill for 4-5 minutes to melt the cheese.

Chips n' dip

Cover all bases and taste buds by leaving out a bowl of plain tortilla chips with various dips such as guacamole, sour cream etc.

139

Popcorn cake - Easy

For each layer you will need:
50g (2oz) butter or margarine
50g (2oz) caster sugar
1 medium egg
50g (2oz) self raising flour

For decorating:
125g (5oz) butter/margarine
250g (10oz) icing sugar
100g (4oz) red fondant
Popcorn

1. Preheat the oven to 180°c, 350°f, gas mark 4. Grease a 5 inch round cake tin, and line the bottom.

2. Cream the butter and sugar until light and fluffy. Beat in the egg, and then gently fold in the flour.

3. Pour into the prepared tin, and bake for 30-35 minutes. The cake is fully cooked when a skewer inserted in the centre comes out clean. Repeat until you have 4 layers.

4. To make the buttercream - cream the butter, gradually add the icing sugar, and cream together.

5. Using a cake cutting wire, or bread knife, slice the top off each cake to give you a level surface

6. Use a blob of buttercream to stick the cake to the board. Cover the top with a generous amount of buttercream, then add the 2nd cake, cut side down. Repeat until you have sandwiched and stacked all 4 cakes.

7. Cover the entire cake in a thin layer of buttercream and chill in the fridge for 30 minutes. This will seal the cake and stop crumbs mixing in with the final layer.

8. Once set, remove from the fridge and cover the sides with the remaining buttercream to a smooth finish.

9. Thinly roll out the red fondant, and cut into long strips, about 3cm wide. Stick these to the sides of the cake, trimming at the top to fit. *Optional:* Cut an oval from the fondant and stamp with the word popcorn. Stick this to the front of the cake with a little edible glue or water.

10. Top the cake with popcorn.

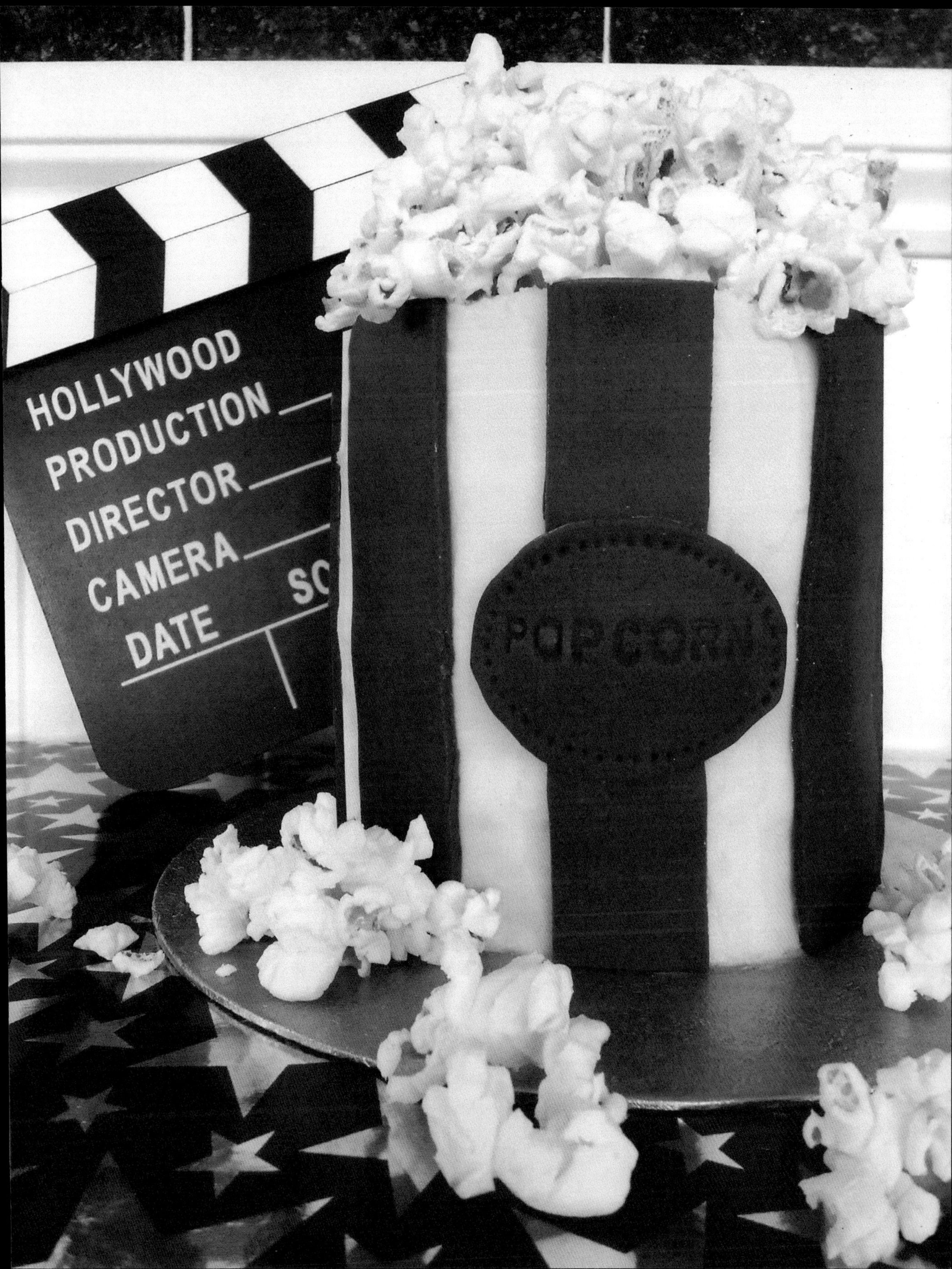
HOLLYWOOD
PRODUCTION
DIRECTOR
CAMERA
DATE
POPCORN

Movie Reel – For the experienced baker

You will need:

200g (8oz) butter or margarine
200g (8oz) caster sugar
4 medium eggs
200g (8oz) self raising flour

For decorating:

100g (4oz) icing sugar
200g (8oz) butter/margarine
500g (20oz) white fondant
500g (20oz) black fondant
Optional:
Food colouring
Cake wire

1. Preheat the oven to 180°c, 350°f, gas mark 4. Grease two 7 inch round tins, and line the bottoms.

2. Cream the butter and sugar until light and fluffy. Beat in the eggs, and then gently fold in the flour.

3. Pour into the prepared tins, and bake for 40-45 minutes. The cake is fully cooked when a skewer inserted in the centre comes out clean.

4. Knead 200g of the white fondant with 100g of the black fondant until you have a nice even mix of colour.

5. Roll the grey out to a thickness of about 5mm. Using an 8 inch tin as a guide, cut 2 large circles.

6. To make the buttercream - cream the butter, gradually add the icing sugar, and cream together.

7. Stick one of the grey circles to the cake board with a little buttercream.

8. Take the other grey circle, and indent as shown left - a large circle just inside the edge, and 4 small circles in the centre. With a cutter, remove the centre of each small circle. Leave this out to air dry.

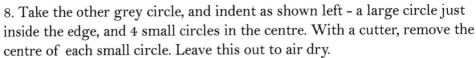

9. Using a cake cutting wire or bread knife, slice the top off each cake to give a flat level surface. Stick in the centre of the fondant base with a little buttercream. Spread the top with a generous amount of buttercream and sandwich the 2nd cake on top - cut side down.

10. Cover the whole cake in a thin layer of buttercream..

Continued.....

  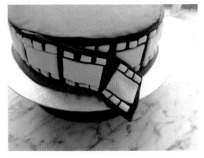

11. Thinly roll out the black fondant, and cut using the 7 inch cake tin as a template. Stick this to the top of the cake.

12. Measure the height of the cake, and cut the black into strips of this height. You will find it much easier to get onto the cake using 3 strips instead of one long one.

13. Now for the fiddly part! Roll out the white fondant, and cut into the large (approx. 40mm x 25mm) and small (approx. 7mm x 7mm) squares that will make up your film roll.

14. Paint a little edible glue or water onto the back of these (one at a time) and stick to the black strips as shown above.

15. When you have completed all 3 strips, carefully stick them to the sides of the cake. Butt each strip together, and apply a little glue where the strips overlap at the front. Leave the excess on - shaping with your fingers so that it falls away from the cake.

Optional but effective: Take the grey circle that we set aside earlier. Cover your work surface and spray with edible silver shimmer spray.

16. Paint a little edible glue or water to the edges of the top of the cake, and carefully place on the top grey circle.

17. Take the remaining white fondant and split into 3. Knead colouring into each, and roll and stamp with a small star cutter. Feed cake wire into these, and push into the top of the cake.

Party bags

Keep the theme going right through to the end with these fabulous movie party bags. All you need are some popcorn boxes to fill with treats!

Pick from movie related treats such as:
• Chocolate bars
• Microwave popcorn sachets
• Popcorn cones
• Pick & mix sweets
• Photo booth style props
• Dress up accessories

You could also re-cover your chocolate bars (as shown right) by making your own wrapper label to your own personal message.

Pyjama Party

A pyjama party doesn't necessarily have to mean a sleepover. This party has been designed with lots of silly fun games with pyjamas as the dress code.

If you are ready to take the plunge and have friends stay overnight keep the number small, sticking only to very close friends. Whichever way you decide to take your party make sure you are specific on the invitation!

The invitation

You will find the template for these invitations ready to download from **www.gemmadenham.com**. Simply type (or write) on your details, and print on a good quality paper.

Voila!

147

The Games

Fantastically silly and sure to have everyone in a giggle! These games are simple to play and highly competitive!

~Stomp~

Blow up a balloon for each child, and tie around one of their ankles. When the music starts they must run round trying to stomp (and pop) each others balloon whilst keeping their own. The last player with a balloon wins!

~Blow out~

Each player has a balloon and a row of cups. Line up the cups along the edge of a table. Each player has to blow the balloon up, then let the air out along the row of cups to knock them off. Players can inflate the balloon as many times as they want - the 1st player to knock over all their cups wins.

~Crazy feet~

Sit everyone in a circle. Blindfold each player, and drop a load of socks into the middle of the circle. The object of the game is to find and put on as many socks as possible onto 1 foot within a set time (or until the socks run out!). The winner is the player wearing the most socks.

~Magic carpet~

For this game you will need 2 hand towels and a hard floor. Divide your party into 2 and play this as a relay. Each player sits on a towel - with their bottoms at the back, and their feet on the front. The idea is to race to the other end of the room by stretching and bending your knees in a 'bum shuffle'. 1st team to cross all their players wins.

~Balloon race~

Each player has a different coloured balloon and a piece of thick card. The object of the game is to get your balloon to the other end of the room by fanning it with the card. Play all together or as a relay depending on your space.

~Cotton nose~

Each player has a plate of cotton wool balls and an empty bowl. Get each player to dab some petroleum jelly onto their noses. With hands behind their backs, the object is to move all the cotton wool from the plate into the bowl using just their noses.

The Food

Midnight feast type food provides the ideal choice for a pyjama party.
Sandwiches and crisps, fruit kebabs and popcorn, and milk/milkshakes and cookies. Perfect!

Sandwich Rolls

Presenting the sandwiches in a different way makes them that little bit more special.

Fillings that work well for these are ham (1 slice per roll), cheese grated with a fine grater, and anything spreadable like jam, cheese spread, peanut butter etc.

1. Cut the crusts off the bread.
2. Lightly roll each slice with a rolling pin. *You are looking to compress the bread slightly so that it will roll without cracking, rather than to flatten it.*
3. Butter the bread, and top with a thin layer of your chosen filling.
4. Roll the bread up, and cut in half.

Make sure to serve these open side down to prevent them from unrolling.

Chocolate Chip Cookies

3-4 tbsp vegetable oil

75g (3oz) sugar

4 tbsp self raising flour

2 tsp baking powder

100g (4oz) plain flour

1 egg

50g (2oz) chocolate chips

Few drops vanilla essence

1. Preheat the oven to 180°c, 350°f, gas mark 4 and grease a baking tray.
2. In a bowl, mix the dry ingredients together.
3. Add the egg, oil and vanilla. Stir well.
4. Roll the mixture into golf ball sized shapes, place onto the baking tray, and pat to flatten.
5. Bake for 15-20 minutes.

Pinata cake - Easy

For the bottom layer:
175g (6oz) butter or margarine
175g (6oz) caster sugar
3 medium eggs
175g (6oz) self raising flour

For the top layer:
100g (4oz) butter or margarine
100g (4oz) caster sugar
2 medium egg
100g (4oz) self raising flour

For decorating:
125g (5oz) butter/margarine
250g (10oz) icing sugar
Sprinkles
Sweets

1. Preheat the oven to 180°c, 350°f, gas mark 4.
Grease two 6 inch round cake tins, and line the bottom.

2. Cream the butter and sugar until light and fluffy. Beat in the eggs, and then gently fold in the flour.

3. Pour into the prepared tins, and bake for 40-45 minutes. The cake is fully cooked when a skewer inserted in the centre comes out clean.

4. To make the buttercream - cream the butter, gradually add the icing sugar, and cream together.

5. Using a cake cutting wire, or bread knife, slice the top off each cake to give you a level surface.

6. Take the bottom cake (the deepest one) and cut a circle from the centre. Spread the bottom with a little buttercream to stick it to the cake board, then cover the top with a generous amount of buttercream. Fill the hole with sweets.

7. Take the top cake, and cover the top with buttercream. Pour the sprinkles onto a plate, and push the cake into them so that they stick to the buttercream.

8. Place the top onto the bottom cake, and cover the sides with a thin layer of buttercream. Refrigerate for 30 minutes, then cover with the remaining buttercream.

Drip cake - Moderate

For the bottom layer:
350g (12oz) butter or margarine
350g (12oz) caster sugar
6 medium egg
350g (12oz) self raising flour
25g (2oz) cocoa powder

For decorating:
125g (5oz) butter/margarine
250g (10oz) icing sugar
150g (6oz) chocolate
Sprinkles

1. Preheat the oven to 180°c, 350°f, gas mark 4. Grease two 6 inch round cake tins, and line the bottom.

2. Cream the butter and sugar until light and fluffy. Beat in the eggs, and then gently fold in the flour.

3. Pour into the prepared tins, and bake for 40-45 minutes. The cake is fully cooked when a skewer inserted in the centre comes out clean.

4. To make the buttercream - cream the butter, gradually add the icing sugar, and cream together.

5. Using a cake cutting wire, or bread knife, slice the top off each cake to give you a flat, level surface.

6. Use a blob of buttercream to stick the cake to the board. Cover the top with a generous amount of buttercream, then add the 2nd cake, cut side down.

7. Cover the entire cake in a thin layer of buttercream, then refrigerate for at least 30 minutes. This will set the buttercream and stop crumbs mixing in with the final finish.

8. Once set, cover the sides of the cake with the remaining buttercream.

9. Break the chocolate into pieces, and melt in a bowl set over a pan of simmering water. Allow to cool slightly, then using a spoon, pour onto the top of cake allowing to drip over the edges. Finish with sprinkles.

Party bags

How fabulous are these for party bags! Sweet, cute, and oh so yummy. Simply fill disposable wine glasses 3/4 of the way up with colourful sweets, and top with a cupcake.

Making cupcakes

100g (4oz) butter
100g (4oz) caster sugar
2 medium eggs
100g (4oz) self raising flour

1. Preheat the oven to 190°c, gas mark 5.
2. Cream the butter and sugar until light and fluffy. Beat in the eggs, and then gently fold in the flour.
3. Pour into 12 paper cases and bake for 15-20 minutes.
4. Once cool, swirl a little buttercream on each cake, and top with a cherry.

Pizza Party

YOU ARE INVITED TO
AMELIA'S
PIZZA PARTY!
~~~
ON FRIDAY 25TH NOVEMBER
5-7PM

AT AMELIA'S HOUSE

R.S.V.P 01234567891

PIZZA PARTY

The invitation

This pizza box invitation certainly has the wow factor! A little time consuming to make but very simple, and what an impact it makes!

The decorations

Turn your space into a pizza parlour with a few simple signs and restaurant accessories - tablecloths, cutlery, menus and condiments all add to the feel.

Making the pizza box invitation

The pizza box template can be found and downloaded from **www.gemmadenham.com**. There are 2 different files to choose from - If you have access to a printer that can print onto card, use the file without measurements. Print the box directly onto A4 card, 1 per invite.

If your printer can't process card, use the file with measurements. Print it out onto paper, then copy it onto card. Again, you will need 1 sheet per invite.

1. Cut the card along all the solid lines.

2. Score, and fold along the dotted lines.

3. Glue (or use double sided tape) on all the tabs, and stick these to the sides to create the box. The central tabs stick onto the bottom, deeper section of the box.

4. To create the pizza, you will need brown paper/card cut into a 10cm diameter circle. A wiggly circle of red paper slightly smaller to be the tomato sauce, and a wiggly circle smaller again to be the cheese. Cut toppings such as red circles for pepperoni, pink squares for ham etc and stick these all together.

5. Glue the pizza into the base of the box. In the lid, type and print, or write the invitation details.

6. Download and print out the pizza box lid, cut and stick into place on the outside of the box.

The Games

Obviously the main activity for a pizza party is going to be the pizza making,
but whilst the pizzas cook keep everyone entertained with a few games.

~Pizza making~

The below dough recipe will make 4 bases. Provide each child with a ball of dough to roll out,
and line the table with bowls of toppings for them to choose from. Continue the culinary fun at
the end of the party by having make your own ice cream sundaes! Yum!

200g plain flour,
10ml easy blend yeast,
1 tbsp oil,
100ml warm water,

1. Sieve the flour into a bowl and mix with the salt and yeast.
2. Add the oil and water, and stir with a knife to form a dough.
3. Knead on a floured surface for 10 minutes.
4. Cut into 4, return to the bowl, and cover with a clean tea towel until needed.

~Pin the moustache on the chef~

Print out, draw or paint a large chef picture, and 1 moustache per child. Stick the chef onto
the wall within easy reach of the children, and stick some double sided tape to the back of the
moustaches. Blindfold each child in turn, and get them to stick their moustache onto the chef.
The player with the moustache in the nearest correct position wins.

~Balloon Relay~

Line up two teams at the end of the room, and two chairs at the opposite end. The 1st player
in line places a balloon between their legs. They then have to run to the other end of the room
(with the balloon between their legs), around the chair, and back again, passing the balloon to
the next in line. The 1st team to complete wins.

~Hot pizza~

Gather everyone into a circle. Whilst the music plays, pass the 'pizza' (this can be a ball,
beanbag or your own fake pizza creation). Keep the 'pizza' moving, and out of your hands. If
the music stops and it's in your hands - you're out!

~Head foam~

This is a very funny game sure to have everyone in the giggles!
Have your players line up in 2 lines facing each other. One line puts on shower caps, which are
then covered in shaving foam. The other line each has a bowl full of cheesy ball crisps. The
object of the game is to throw the crisps to the person opposite you - who has to catch them on
their head! The player with the most crisps on their head at the end wins.

Pizza cake - *Easy*

You will need:
100g (4oz) butter or margarine
100g (4oz) caster sugar
2 medium eggs
100g (4oz) self raising flour

For decorating:
25g (1oz) butter/margarine
50g (2oz) icing sugar
Red food colouring
75g (3oz) white chocolate
Licorice ribbon 1x red 1x green
1 black licorice rope
2 red fruit strips
3 mushroom sweets

This has to be the quickest and easiest cake I have ever made, and it looks stunning!

1. Preheat the oven to 180°c, 350°f, gas mark 4. Grease an 8 inch round cake tin, and line the bottom.

2. Cream the butter and sugar until light and fluffy. Beat in the eggs, and then gently fold in the flour.

3. Pour into the prepared tin, and bake for 40-45 minutes. The cake is fully cooked when a skewer inserted in the centre comes out clean.

4. To make the buttercream - cream the butter, gradually add the icing sugar and food colouring, and cream together. Spread over the top of the cake - but not all the way to the edge. This is to look like sauce.

5. Take the white chocolate, and 'grate' with a vegetable peeler (you will find this easier than using a grater!). Sprinkle over the 'sauce'.

6. For the pepperoni - take the fruit strips and cut with a small circular cutter.

7. With the licorice ribbon - use the red cut into squares to make ham, and use the green cut into strips to make pepper.

8. Cut the liquorice rope into slices, then using a fine piping nozzle, cut small circles out of the centre. These should now look like olives.

9. Cut the mushroom sweets in half, and arrange all the toppings on the pizza.

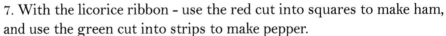
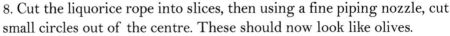
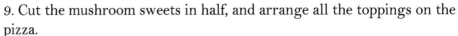

Party bags

Keep the party bags simple with these take-out bags. All you need are some white paper bags. The thank you panel (shown left) can be downloaded and printed out from **www.gemmadenham.com**.

Chose and pick what to fill your bags with from cooking related accessories such as:

- Chef's hat
- Mini rolling pin
- Cookie cutters
- Stick on chef's moustache
- Measuring spoons
- Apron
- Recipe cards
- Pastry brush

How to...

Make a pinata

1. A balloon creates the easiest shape, but you can make any shape you wish so long as you start with a hollow shape. To make a more elaborate shape, tape cardboard onto your base shape.

2. Make up your papier mache paste by mixing equal amounts of plain flour and water.

3. Tear newspaper into strips. Dip into the paste and remove any excess. Stick to the balloon in a criss-cross pattern until the balloon is covered - all but a hole for filling!

4. Leave to dry, then repeat until you have built up 3 or 4 layers. Leave to dry out completely, then pop and remove the balloon.

5. For a traditional pinata - glue crepe paper strips onto your shape as below. Alternatively, paint your pinata in your chosen design.

6. Punch two holes in the top of your pinata, and tie string or ribbon to create a loop. Fill with wrapped sweets (remember these will be hitting the floor!) or small toys, stickers or confetti.

7. Cover the hole with tape or paper, and paint if required. Attach some string to the loop and hang.

Cover a cake in fondant icing

1. Prepare your cake. Using a cake cutting wire, or bread knife, slice the top off the cake to give you a flat, level top. If using more than one layer of cake, sandwich together with a generous amount of buttercream.

2. Measure across the top and sides of the cake using a piece of string. This will act as a guide when you roll the icing out later.

3. Use a good blob of buttercream to stick the cake to the cake board, and cover the entire cake with a thin layer of buttercream - Pile it on top of the cake and ease it across the top and sides. Be sure to fill all the gaps when smoothing it. Leave it in the fridge to firm for 30 minutes.

4. Make sure your work surface is clean and free of any crumbs. Dust with icing sugar, and knead the fondant for a few minutes until pliable.

5. Roll out the fondant to fit the cake, using the string for guidance. Lift the icing using a rolling pin or your hands, and drape it over the top of the cake.

6. Smooth the fondant with your hands pulling out any creases and smoothing down from the top.

7. Use a small knife to cut away the excess icing – don't cut too close to the cake! For a perfect finish run over the cake with two cake smoothers.

With thanks

First of all I need to say a huge thank you to all the wonderful children who took part in the making of this book. Charlie Baker, Jack Baker, Edward Bates, Emily Bates, Edward Black, Jacob Blount, George Cotterill, Nancy Ellis, William Ellis, Luke Faulknall, Georgina Faulknall, Aimee Gertse, Archie Gibbons, Harvey Griffiths, Rylee Grindall, Maddison Hadfield, Emily Hibberd, Thomas Hibberd, Kora Nevitt, Iona Slorach, Lochlainn Slorach, Freya Szulczewski, George Szulczewski, Sophie Turner, William Turner, and Alfie Venables. I truly could not have made this book without you all, you were absolutely fantastic!

My second thanks goes out to all of their parents, my wonderful friends, for letting them appear in the book, and for their fantastic support and encouragement. I love you all dearly, and I really do appreciate everything you have done to help me along the way!

Further thanks goes out to my incredible family for their ongoing support in my work. Thank you to Jon and Sam Page for their use of props, thanks to Gordon for his special appearance, thanks to Steve Page for the use of his camera equipment and thanks to Carol Page for her editing. Also, as joint editor, a big thank you to Rebecca Slorach.

Last but by no means least, special thanks goes out to my son Joshua Denham. Inspiration for so much of my work, and without whom, this book would not have come about.

Gemma Denham x

Index

Printed in Great Britain
by Amazon